The Best Bourbon You'll Never Taste

The Best Bourbon You'll Never Taste

The True Story Of
A. H. Hirsch Reserve
Straight Bourbon Whiskey,
Distilled In The Spring Of 1974

By Charles K. Cowdery

Chicago, Illinois

For information about this book, write or call:

Made and Bottled in Kentucky
PMB 298, 3712 N. Broadway
Chicago, IL 60613-4198
773-477-9691
cowdery@ix.netcom.com
http://www.bourbonstraight.com

The Best Bourbon You'll Never Taste. The True Story Of A. H. Hirsch Reserve Straight Bourbon Whiskey, Distilled In The Spring Of 1974

First printing 2012.

ISBN 978-0-9758703-1-0

Library of Congress Control Number: 2012946217

CONTENTS:

1. Preface.

This is the print edition of a book originally published as an ebook in April, 2012. That book was, in the main, a new work but it was based on a feature published in two parts in *The Bourbon Country Reader,* Volume 9, Numbers 5 and 6, released in August and October of 2006. The headline for the first installment was: "Mystery; the 253-Year Story of A. H. Hirsch 'Pot Still' Bourbon." The second headline was: "Part II: A. H. Hirsch, the Man, the Mystery and the Whiskey."

Anyone familiar with those articles will see immediately that the present work has been updated and expanded significantly, but the core of those articles remains. Factually, both articles are sound and nothing in this work refutes them.

Some of the information contained herein was discovered after that 2006 publication. In particular, there is extensive material provided by Dick Stoll, who worked at Michter's from 1955 until it closed on, as he vividly recalls, February 14, 1990.

The Bourbon Country Reader is a newsletter about American whiskey. Always independent and idiosyncratic, it accepts no advertising and is not affiliated with any whiskey producer. The ebook upon which this print edition is based is the second publication derived from past issues of *The Reader* and, assuming it does well, there will be more.

This is my alternative to making *The Reader* itself available online.

You can always learn about new print and ebook releases by following The Chuck Cowdery blog at http://www.bourbonstraight.com.

Subscriptions to the newsletter are $20/year for U.S. addresses, $24.50 for Canada, and $28.50 for everybody else. *The Bourbon Country Reader* is published six times a year. (Well, maybe not, but your subscription always includes six issues.) It is produced and delivered the old-fashioned way; ink on paper, in an envelope, delivered personally to your home or office by a uniformed representative of the United States government. Subscription rates are subject to change without notice.

Since I began to write about American whiskey about 20 years ago, many people have referred to me as a bourbon historian. I usually resist that label because real historians rely on original research. In most of my work, I am more of a history writer, i.e., one who relies primarily on secondary sources. In this case, I am more the former than I have ever been, working to a large extent from interviews with principals or people who knew them, and from original documents. It is exciting to uncover previously unknown information.

Much of the information in this book has never been published anywhere before.

The story of A. H. Hirsch Reserve is a story about business, about how businesses and business conditions can change, and it is a story about passion bordering on obsession, a condition for which each individual finds a different kind of release. Researching, documenting, and telling the true story of this unique whiskey as well as I can is my outlet.

This is the story of A. H. Hirsch Reserve Straight Bourbon Whiskey so it is, inevitably, the story of the Pennsylvania distillery where that whiskey was made. That would be an interesting story even if the A. H. Hirsch Reserve bourbon had never happened, but not nearly *as* interesting.

When the Hirsch bourbons were first discovered by enthusiasts and ultimately deemed exceptional, very little was known about their true provenance. People in the distribution channel – the producers, distributors, and retailers who handled the product in its various iterations – shared what little they knew and, sometimes, made things up to fill in the gaps. Little by little, the real story has come out. This is the first time it has been told with this level of reliability and detail.

-- CKC, August 2012

2. It Can Be Done.

As this is being written, early in 2012, it is not impossible to still taste this legendary bourbon. If tasting A. H. Hirsch Reserve Straight Bourbon Whiskey is something you are determined to do, the task likely will be difficult, probably frustrating, and almost certainly expensive, but it can be done.

There are many (no one knows how many) bottles in private collections in the United States, Japan, and other countries. Reportedly, and there is no way to confirm this, a few people still have cases of it. You can be pretty sure that most of them know how rare, desirable, and potentially valuable it is.

There are even a few bottles (again, actual numbers are unknown) still available for sale in retail stores. Sightings are reported from time to time. A handful of bars around the country still sell it by the drink, though again it is impossible to list them or even guess how much they are charging for it now. As of this writing, Delilah's in Chicago still has the 16-year-old gold capsule bottling on its back bar.

In February of 2012, a bottle of A. H. Hirsch Reserve was purchased at a small liquor store in Louisville, Kentucky, for its original price of $43.95. That sort of thing is very uncommon, but it happens.

It's peculiar, but since whiskey doesn't change in the bottle, either for better or worse, some retailers never clear out old inventory. They also don't take inventory, so they don't even know what they have. A whole subset of bourbon enthusiasts, called 'dusty hunters,' is made possible by this fact. They sometimes find bottles that have been on a shelf for decades.

That bottle found in February was likely there for five years or more. It can't be reordered. The producer doesn't have any more of it and neither do the distributors. Except for the odd bottle here and there at retail, it's all gone.

You may see A. H. Hirsch Reserve for sale on eBay or similar services. Just be aware that most eBay sellers are not licensed alcohol retailers and it is a serious violation of both state and federal law to sell alcoholic beverages without a license. Contrary to what eBay implies, there is no exception for collectible bottles with 'incidental' contents. You may not be breaking any laws as the buyer but the person selling you the whiskey almost certainly is.

The legal consequence of buying alcoholic beverages from an unlicensed seller is less clear and varies by state. In some states, it is illegal to ship or accept shipments of alcoholic beverages if you do not have the appropriate license. Only producers, distributors, and retailers can get licenses. Ordinary consumers cannot.

This doesn't make it impossible to purchase a bottle of beverage alcohol from a private individual, it just makes it difficult and risky. If the seller screws you, good luck appealing to law enforcement for help since the transaction was illegal to begin with.

When prices of anything old and rare get to a certain point, someone will try to counterfeit the desired object. It has happened with old single malts scotches, The Macallan in particular. There have been no reported cases of counterfeit bottles of A. H. Hirsch Reserve being sold, but it's always possible.

If you think you have located an authentic bottle, the words to look for are 'A. H. Hirsch Reserve Straight Bourbon Whiskey.' All of them. In particular, beware of products labeled "Hirsch" without the initials "A. H." They may be perfectly good whiskey, they just are not this whiskey.

A word about whiskey labels. All beverage alcohol labels must be approved by a federal government agency, the Treasury Department's Tax and Trade Bureau. Many states require approval from a state agency as well. Some words are regulated and some are not. 'Regulated,' in this case, means a product has to have certain characteristics if the producer wants to use certain words to describe it. Whiskey, for example, is a distilled spirit made from grain and aged in wood containers. A straight whiskey is one that has been aged for at least two years in new, charred oak containers. Bourbon is a whiskey made primarily from corn and aged in new, charred oak containers. And so on. The terms 'whiskey,' 'straight,' and 'bourbon' are all regulated.

The term 'reserve' is not. Nor are the terms 'sour mash' and 'pot still.' They aren't regulated and, therefore, aren't required to be true.

A. H. Hirsch Reserve Straight Bourbon Whiskey began in 1989. There have been 20-year-old, 19-year-old, 18-year-old, 16-year-old and 15-year-old expressions sold. They are all the same whiskey, just withdrawn from the barrels at different times.

While we are on the subject of labels, age statements must refer to the youngest whiskey in the bottle. If the label says "16 Years Old," then the youngest whiskey in the bottle must be at least 16 years old. There may be older whiskey in the bottle, but not younger whiskey.

The first few bottlings of A. H. Hirsch Reserve, at 15-years-old, were very small and most of that went to Japan. The 15-, 18- and 19-year-olds have always been extremely rare. The 20-year-old is slightly more common, but only in the bunkers of its many fans. It has been years since a bottle of it has shown up at retail.

The last and far-and-away largest release was the 16-year-old topped with a gold foil capsule, like the one recently bought in Kentucky. That bottling was released in 2003 at a retail price of about $45 a bottle. In mid-2006, the producer reported that he was down to his last 1,000 cases. In 2009, everything that was left was rebottled in fancy decanters priced at $1,500 each.

Since their release, the decanters have come down a little in price. The bottles are rarely seen for less than $350 each.

The producer for both of those releases was Preiss Imports (Now part of Anchor Brewing). Unless they still have a few of the $1,500 decanters left, that's it. The whiskey is all gone and so is the distillery where it was made.

This book is the story of how a $45 bottle of bourbon became a legend.

3. Pennsylvania Pride.

All of the A. H. Hirsch Reserve bourbons are very good and they come with an intriguing story, always a winning combination.

Unfortunately, depending on which story you've heard, some of it is not true.

Fortunately, the true story is more interesting, and more than interesting enough to make up for the falsehoods.

The best-known version goes like this. In the spring of 1974 a batch of bourbon whiskey was distilled in Pennsylvania at a small distillery near Schaefferstown. The distillery went out of business and the whiskey was 'rescued.' Some was bottled and sold right away and the rest was allowed to continue aging in Kentucky.

In the early 1990s, the A. H. Hirsch Reserve brand was created to market this whiskey, primarily in Japan. It was always a small, exclusive brand. Demand for it was tempered by its high price. The cost varied, especially as certain expressions became scarce, but even before it became the impossible-to-find legend it is now it was, at $45 to $100+ a bottle, among the costliest American whiskeys on the market.

As the story goes, a former executive of Schenley Distillers Corporation acquired the whiskey initially and launched the brand. His name was Adolph Hirsch and he named the product after himself. It then passed from him to Gordon Hue, whose family owns the Cork-and-Barrel liquor stores in Covington, Kentucky (just across the river from Cincinnati). From him it passed to Henry Preiss and his company, Preiss Imports, in San Diego, California.

That story is all anyone knew until a few years ago, when writers observing the phenomenon that A. H. Hirsch Reserve had become began to investigate its origins more diligently.

They learned that the Pennsylvania distillery was called Michter's and it made a whiskey called Michter's Original Sour Mash. Was Michter's Original Sour Mash the same stuff as A. H. Hirsch Reserve?

No, it was not.

What about the Michter's bourbon, rye and other whiskeys on store shelves today? What's that and what is its relationship to the Michter's Distillery and A. H. Hirsch Reserve Bourbon?

After Michter's closed, the Michter's trademark was abandoned. A few years later, a Philadelphia company called Chatham Imports re-registered the abandoned mark and began to sell a line of Michter's bourbons and other whiskeys. None of the whiskey they sell was made at the Michter's Distillery in Pennsylvania. They are a non-distiller producer, which means they buy bulk whiskey made by one or more of the usual suspects and bottle it under the Michter's brand name.

Because they control rights to the Michter's name, they can and do claim what is now (as of 2012) 259 years of Michter's history as their own, even though they have just the name and nothing else that connects them to the distillery in Schaefferstown. Ironically, the Michter's name itself is only about 60 years old. Over the years, the distillery was known by many different names.

In 2011, the new Michter's announced its intention to build a micro-distillery in downtown Louisville, and they joined the Kentucky Distillers Association. That Michter's had nothing to do with A. H. Hirsch Reserve and has no further role in its story.

Michter's, it turns out, was not primarily a distillery. It was a brand name, used for a product called Michter's Original Sour Mash Whiskey. That product was sold for about 40 years beginning in the 1950s. It was made at the distillery in Schaefferstown that also made the A. H. Hirsch Reserve, but from a different recipe. The marketing company that sold Michter's Original Sour Mash Whiskey was called Michter's Jug House.

There was always a connection between that company and the Schaefferstown distillery. The Schaefferstown distillery posed as the Michter's Distillery for many years when its actual name was Pennco. The distillery was only named Michter's for about 15 years, the last 15 of its existence (1975-1990). It has come to be known by that name in part because it was the final name, and in part because those years were marked by an emphasis on tourism, so the Michter's name was heavily publicized.

Prior to 1975, the official location of the Michter's Jug House company was Sheridan, Pennsylvania, an even tinier community about seven miles northeast of Schaefferstown, just west of Newmanstown.

The whiskey sold as Michter's from the 1950s through the 1980s was not bourbon. Nor was it rye, the whiskey style usually associated with Pennsylvania. It was mostly corn but not quite enough to be called bourbon. The rest was rye and barley malt. It was disqualified from being called straight whiskey because at least some used barrels were employed for its aging. It didn't carry an age statement but was probably four to five years old. It was not a blended whiskey. It was an original creation made only by that distillery.

At some point in the 1960s, Michter's began to emulate Jack Daniel's. Jack Daniel's Tennessee Whiskey, owned by Brown Forman, has been one of America's top whiskey brands since the 1950s and widely copied. Michter's in the 1960s was sold in a square bottle with a white-on-black label, like Jack Daniel's, and later advertising mentioned Jack Daniel's in an attempt to position Michter's as similar, another proud not-from-Kentucky, non-bourbon whiskey. Michter's was the last whiskey distillery in Pennsylvania, which had once been America's leading whiskey producer.

Michter's Original Sour Mash Whiskey was essentially a local product, made in Pennsylvania and sold primarily to Pennsylvanians.

Michter's also copied Jack Daniel's by using the words 'Sour Mash' on its label. Every major brand of American-made whiskey is sour mash whiskey, most just don't choose to include those words on their packaging.

Unlike Jack Daniel's, which in all respects is made exactly like bourbon, Michter's mixed whiskey aged in new barrels with whiskey aged in re-used barrels. This was done to reduce cost and give the product a lighter, milder taste. Early Times Kentucky Whisky, a popular brand today that's made by Brown Forman, uses the same technique.

Over the years, the whiskey sold by Michter's Jug House was sold in white ceramic crocks, square glass bottles, round glass bottles, and collectible decanters in a variety of designs. The busts of King Tut and Queen Nefertiti are particularly sharp.

Most of the Michter's whiskey that still shows up for sale is in the collectible decanters. Whiskey doesn't spoil so old whiskey in sealed glass bottles can keep indefinitely. Ceramic is more porous, and the closures aren't usually as tight, so oxidation damage is a risk. Excessive oxidation doesn't make whiskey harmful, but it does make it taste bad.

Although it has been more than 20 years since the last Michter's whiskey was released, it's not impossible to find a bottle or decanter stuck in the corner of a dusty, old liquor store.

When A. H. Hirsch Reserve first became popular, many people assumed (incorrectly, it turns out) that any whiskey made at Michter's was either the same whiskey or comparable to it. A lot of the remaining Michter's stock was bought up with that in mind.

The people who bought it weren't necessarily disappointed – Michter's made good whiskey – but they didn't get A. H. Hirsch Reserve. The Hirsch whiskey was bourbon, the Michter's was not. The Hirsch bourbon was at least 15-years-old, the Michter's wasn't a third that.

The last producer to market A. H. Hirsch Reserve bourbon, the company that ultimately sold most of it, was Preiss Imports, a small company out of San Diego that was, as the name implies, primarily an importer of wines and spirits, including the revered Springbank Single Malt Scotch.

In 2008, Preiss Imports was acquired by the Griffin Group, which subsequently bought Anchor Brewery and Distillery, and merged Anchor with Preiss to form Anchor Brewers & Distillers, LLC. Anchor makes Anchor Steam beer and Old Potrero whiskey. They still import Springbank and other scotches. They have a strong portfolio.

Henry Preiss, the founder of Preiss Imports, is still employed by the company. Fritz Maytag, who previously owned Anchor, has retired.

Anchor still sells whiskey under the Hirsch name, but without the initials 'A. H.' They don't disclose the sources of those whiskeys, but none of it was made at the distillery in Schaefferstown.

Back when he still owned the company, Henry Preiss promised they would never use the name 'A. H. Hirsch Reserve' again, so people could be sure that anything with that name on it is that whiskey. One hopes the new owners will continue to honor that pledge.

Most of the questions people have about A. H. Hirsch Reserve will be answered in the pages that follow. A few aspects of the story are still difficult to confirm. That Preiss distributed the last of it is certain.

The involvement of the Hue family, which started the brand, is well established but some details are murky. We know about how much there was, when each batch was bottled, and how much was in each batch. We know where it was made, when it was made, how it was made, and who made it.

Adolph Hirsch definitely was a person of importance at the Schenley Distillers Corporation, but he had only a minor role in creating the brand that bears his name. How he came to own a batch of bourbon made in the spring of 1974, and why he did nothing with it for more than a decade, is still unclear.

But many other questions can now be answered.

4. The First 100 Years.

The Michter's Distillery, where the whiskey that became A. H. Hirsch Reserve was made, dates back to 1753.

It had many names: Michter's, Pennco, Kirk's Pure Rye, Bomberger's, Shenk's, and maybe others. The Michter's name was coined in the early 1950s as a brand and applied to the distillery itself only after 1975.

It wasn't the first distillery in America. It was one of many at a time when distilleries were small and whiskey-making was a sideline of farming. It was never the biggest nor the fanciest, nor the most historically significant. That claim belongs to the distillery of America's first president, George Washington, which he operated for several years on his Mount Vernon estate.

Washington grew grain, milled it, and distilled it into whiskey on his Virginia farm. His personal involvement was limited to oversight. His employees and slaves did all the work. His Scottish estate manager, James Anderson, was the main instigator and may have been the Master Distiller.

Washington's distillery operated from 1797 until his death in 1799, and continued intermittently for a few years after that in the hands of others. It was eventually razed.

In 1995, the Commonwealth of Virginia gave the land where the distillery had once stood to Mount Vernon. Virginia had operated a small park on the site, which long ago was detached from the main estate. The park featured a restored grist mill. It was always known that there had been a distillery near the grist mill but no clear trace of it remained. Between 1995 and 2008, the distillery site was identified, studied and excavated, and the distillery was rebuilt. Washington's records pertaining to its operation were also studied. The rebuilt distillery opened to the public in 2008. Much of the funding for the project was contributed by alcoholic beverage interests.

Although Michter's didn't have such a prominent owner, its distinction is that there was a nearly unbroken history of whiskey-making on the same Pennsylvania site for 237 years (1753 to 1990). Few other American distilleries can match that run. Laird's, an applejack maker in New Jersey that is still in operation, claims a 1698 beginning (314 years), but no one else is even close. Jim Beam claims 217 years and counting.

Today, little remains of the distillery once known as Michter's. Successive owners have talked about rebuilding and reopening it, but no one has even come close. Its historic landmark status was revoked years ago. There isn't even a roadside historic marker. For all anyone driving by can tell, it's just another unused piece of land with a few derelict buildings on it.

Shabby, anonymous, forgotten.

Two-hundred and fifty-nine years ago, it was a farm.

In 1753, a Swiss Mennonite named Johann Shenk built a small distillery on his farm near Schaefferstown in what became Lebanon County, Pennsylvania. Many of America's early farmer-distillers were Mennonite immigrants.

George Washington had just turned 21 and been appointed by Virginia Governor Dinwiddie as one of four district adjutants in the Virginia militia, with the rank of major.

If you look for Schaefferstown on a map, it is roughly between Harrisburg and Philadelphia, a little north of Lancaster. It is about ten miles southeast of the city of Lebanon, the county seat. The distillery site isn't actually in Schaefferstown. It is on the outskirts.

Schaefferstown was a small town then and it's a small town still. Its claim to fame is that it has the oldest waterworks in the United States. The city fathers rarely mention its distillery.

Because the distillery has had so many different names, we may in places refer to it as 'Schaefferstown,' 'the Schaefferstown distillery,' or 'the Schaefferstown operation.' Schaefferstown was never part of the distillery's name, but the distillery was always there. However much it changed it only ever had the one location. That's what makes it unique.

When Johann Shenk built the original distillery in 1753, he wasn't unusual. He was, in fact, very much like George Washington except on a smaller scale. Many farmers operated small distilleries on their land. They grew grain which they used to feed their livestock and themselves, and also made into whiskey.

Distilleries in those days weren't licensed. If you wanted to make and sell distilled spirits, there were few restrictions. It was not yet taxed.

Why make whiskey? When most of your neighbors are farmers too, and raise the same crops, there isn't much of a market for grain within your local community. Since transportation then was undeveloped, there was no easy way to get surplus grain to market. Distilling grain into whiskey is a way to prevent it from spoiling, increase its value, and make it easier to transport and trade.

Whiskey is stable. It does not spoil. It is liquid, so it can be transferred in any quantity. It is concentrated, taking up much less space than the grain from which it was made. Because there is always a market for it, and almost everybody uses it, everybody knows how much it is worth. For those reasons, whiskey became virtual currency in the barter-based economy of the American frontier.

Initially, it is likely Shenk just made whiskey for his own household use. A grain farmer's goal is always to harvest more than he needs, a surplus, and distillation was simply the best way to preserve that surplus. Most farmers either distilled or knew someone who did.

Typically when a new part of the American frontier was settled, everyone practiced subsistence farming and was more or less self-sufficient. The next stage was specialization. Since some frontier farmer-distillers were more skilled than others, the best ones became specialists and distilled for their neighbors.

A good whiskey was one that was about 50 percent alcohol-by-volume. With the technology that was available at the time, it took skill to achieve that standard consistently. Good flavor was important too, but secondary; alcohol content was the main thing. The best distillers managed both.

People who wanted to trade whiskey for something else of value had to be able to prove their spirit contained enough spirit. The methods were crude and approximate. One involved mixing a small amount of whiskey with gunpowder and igniting it. If it sputtered and went out, the whiskey didn't contain enough alcohol. If it burned steadily with a clean, blue flame, it was just right. The whiskey was then said to be 'proved' or 'proofed,' and 'proof' (later 'full proof' or '100 proof') became the term for a solution containing 50 percent alcohol and 50 percent water.

Rarely the whiskey/gunpowder mixture would flash out. That meant it was more than 50 percent alcohol and 'over-proof.'

When the best farmer-distillers began to provide distilling services for their neighbors, they would expect to keep about five percent of the neighbor's grain as payment.

To make whiskey from grain, it first has to be coarsely ground into grist. Although some farmers did their own milling, miller was another early specialization among the settlers. This wasn't unique to Pennsylvania. The same pattern was repeated throughout the colonies.

Like the distiller, the miller was paid in grain so millers usually had surplus grist to sell if a distiller needed more. Many millers became distillers themselves but if a miller didn't distill, he likely was glad to trade grist for whiskey with someone who did.

This was basic frontier economics. In this way, a community where everyone began as a self-sufficient farmer would begin to create specialists. Where distilling or milling started out as a farmer's sideline, that business might grow until he became a specialist and either farmed on the side or gave farming up altogether. An eldest son might inherit the family farm and keep farming, while the younger sons became specialists in distilling, milling, or other fields.

Abraham Overholt (1784-1870) is a good example. He grew up on a Pennsylvania farm where his father distilled for the household's use. It was a large family and Abraham was one of the younger children. When he got old enough, running the still became his main job and he began to take in grain from neighbors. As an adult, he transitioned from farming and distilling to just distilling, and began to distill on a commercial scale. His signature brand of rye whiskey, Old Overholt, is still sold.

If a frontier community developed a reputation as a place for good whiskey, the next specialist to set up shop might be a coppersmith, who would be able to make and repair a full range of copper tools and vessels, including the stills and worms used by distillers.

Many rural distilleries in the East achieved commercial scale during and after the American Revolution. It is said that Johann Shenk sold his whiskey to Washington's army. It was, as 20th century advertising would claim, "the whiskey that warmed the Revolution." Militaries in that era issued whiskey (or some other spirit) to troops as part of their daily ration.

Most soldiers and sailors supplemented their ration whenever they could.

Beer, cider and wine were also made and consumed, but they didn't travel well in those days before pasteurization and preservatives so they were usually consumed very close to where they were produced. Whiskey traveled very well and became an article of commerce as well as a popular drink. You might not be able to acquire beer, wine or cider in some places, but you could almost always find whiskey.

In the chronology of Michter's that you usually see, Johann Shenk's great-granddaughter, Elizabeth Shenk Kratzer, sold the distillery to Abraham S. Bomberger in the late 1850s. The Bomberger family operated it until Prohibition. Pennco Distillers, Inc. operated it from Repeal until 1978, then sold the property to Michter's.

The principal source for this chronology, and most of the historical information disseminated by the various producers of A. H. Hirsch Reserve, is Yvonne Bomberger Fowler, a descendant of Abe Bomberger. Parts of it are supported by marketing brochures published by Michter's, though both probably relied on the same original Bomberger family sources. Both Gordon Hue, who created the A. H. Hirsch brand, and Preiss Imports relied primarily on this material for the history they sold along with the whiskey.

Fowler's version is essentially correct but she neglects to mention the role of Louis Forman, a glaring omission, as Forman was in the middle of virtually everything that happened there after 1942. He even coined the Michter's name.

Louis Forman's business records are housed at the Hagley Museum and Library in Wilmington, Delaware. They contain copies of documents dealing with the Bomberger distillery dating back to 1784. The legend is that Forman found these records in October of 1950, in a room that had been sealed shut just before Prohibition began in 1920. They tell a slightly different story than Fowler's.

5. The Whiskey Broker.

Louis Forman was born in Camden, New Jersey, in 1908. His profession prior to 1933 is unknown, but he came of age in the last years of National Prohibition (1920-1933). After Repeal, he entered business as a small-scale liquor broker in Philadelphia, as Louis Forman & Company, Inc., and also did business as the Philadelphia Brokerage Company. The latter business was incorporated in Pennsylvania on July 17, 1941.

Today, most American whiskey is made by companies that both make and market the product, leaving little room for brokers, although they still exist. It was different in Forman's day. Whiskey was considered a commodity. This was even more true before Prohibition. Though the business was changing, there was still a lot of commodity whiskey business going on when Lou Forman got into it in 1933.

In that business, distilleries made bourbon whiskey, rye whiskey, and other spirits, which they sold in bulk to brokers, who sold it in turn to beverage companies who would blend, package and brand the spirit, and then sell it to distributors, who sold it into retail distribution (bars and liquor stores), where it finally was sold to consumers. Whiskey and soap were the first products distributed nationally and marketed using what we now call branding.

It was the beverage companies, sometimes the brokers, but generally not the distilleries, that created and owned most brand names.

As the industry evolved, beverage companies and whiskey brokers often acquired distilleries. It rarely happened the other way around. In that way the industry gradually became vertically integrated.

The industry was always volatile. Distilleries changed hands frequently and most distillery owners owned many, singly or with partners, in the course of their careers. Distillers started most distilleries but rarely held on to them for long, especially after aged whiskey became the standard.

Brokers are typically middle-men who buy and sell but never actually handle the merchandise. The only thing they make is deals. They provide value by giving their customers the exact quantity and quality of whiskey the customer wants, at the price the customer wants to pay, with delivery available when the customer needs it. Brokers make their money by selling for more than they paid. Their capital is at risk but their expenses are low because they never take delivery nor do anything to the product themselves.

Before Prohibition, commodity production was the norm and vertical integration was the exception. When bottling became routine in the early 20th century (before that, whiskey was primarily sold in barrels) the bottling lines were not at the distilleries like they are today, they were at the beverage companies.

As Prohibition approached in 1920, most whiskey wholesalers (whether brokers or beverage companies) were able to sell all of their inventory before the end came. They may have taken a loss, but they sold it. The people who got stuck with whiskey they could not legally sell were the distillers, who still had immature whiskey aging in their warehouses.

Although that aging whiskey lost much of its value on January 17, 1920, it did not become worthless. The Prohibition law offered two windows of opportunity for legal sales. Bakers were permitted to buy a certain amount of rum to make rum cakes, and doctors were permitted to write prescriptions (within defined limits) for whiskey or any other spirit, 'for medicinal use.'

This was not a joke. Many respectable physicians in those days regarded whiskey as an effective general purpose 'tonic,' as a restorative, and a sleep aid. They genuinely regarded it as medicine. That is not to say, however, that every medicinal whiskey prescription written during Prohibition was written for a legitimate medical purpose.

The comparison to our modern experience with medical marijuana is apt.

Because the new law included this limited way for spirits to enter the marketplace legally, it also made it possible for some to be diverted into illegal distribution channels.

Medicinal whiskey prescriptions were written by doctors and filled by pharmacists, who bought the whiskey from companies that had medicinal whiskey licenses issued by the federal government. Licensees were not permitted to make whiskey, so they bought distilleries to obtain aging inventory, or 'barrel stock.'

Initially, the aging whiskey was left where it was made, but it was hard to protect it from theft in remote, rural distilleries, especially when the thieves were often the distillery's owners, or parties acting on their behalf. Eventually a system of consolidation warehouses was established by the Federal government, typically in big cities where the warehouses could be secured and monitored by Treasury agents.

In many cases when medicinal whiskey companies bought whiskey, they also acquired trademark rights to important brand names. Most medicinal whiskey was sold under an established brand name such as Golden Wedding, Old Taylor, George Dickel, Old Grand-Dad, or Old Overholt. Those became the names people remembered after the drought ended while many other once popular brands that were not sold medicinally were forgotten. Before Prohibition, most brands were regional. The major medicinal whiskey brands became nationally known.

Most of the whiskey sold between 1920 and 1933 as medicinal whiskey was distilled and barreled before 1920. Only in 1929 did the government authorize medicinal whiskey companies to begin distilling again, because the whiskey made before 1920 was finally running out.

Selling medicinal whiskey wasn't a great business. People who got into it did so because they believed Prohibition would fail and they would have a head start in the new, legal marketplace.

They were right.

After Repeal, the big medicinal whiskey companies did become the big, vertically integrated whiskey producers and their industry domination gradually eliminated the need for brokers such as Louis Forman, but not right away.

Another factor pushing the trend toward vertical integration was that many distillers from the pre-Prohibition era who wanted to resume distilling after Repeal found themselves with insufficient funds. Because whiskey must age before it can be sold, and because taxes are owed (though not due) as soon as the spirit leaves the still, distilleries need a lot of financing.

After Prohibition, many old-time distillers either rebuilt their old distilleries or built new ones, started producing, then ran out of money and sold out, often to big city wholesalers who had access to financing but needed a reliable source of whiskey. This is how the Jim Beam Distillery came to be owned by Harry Blum, a Chicago whiskey broker; instead of by the Beam family. Similarly, the Old Tom Moore Distillery (today's Barton 1792 Distillery) was rebuilt by Tom Moore's son but he sold it and it eventually came to be owned by Oscar Getz and Lester Abelson, also Chicago whiskey brokers. T. W. Samuels, the distillery built by the Samuels family (later of Maker's Mark fame), came to be controlled by a New York outfit.

Distilleries were losing their independence but, in the process, a new and more stable business model was being created.

While making a survey of licensed American distilleries in 1937, Louis Forman happened upon a small distillery in Schaefferstown, Lebanon County, Pa., which dated back to the mid-eighteenth century.

The word 'licensed' is significant. That Forman's records say the Schaefferstown distillery was licensed in 1937 is one of the few pieces of evidence to support a date that early for its return to production after Prohibition.

Forman's records tell a more detailed story about the distillery's chain of ownership than Fowler's do. They say that at Johann Shenk's death the distillery passed to his daughter and son-in-law, John Kratzer. It remained in the Kratzer family until 1861 when Abraham Bomberger purchased it. He was not, however, a completely disinterested party. He was family too, married to Elizabeth Shenk Kratzer, Johann Shenk's great-grandaughter.

Because ownership passed through the daughters there were several surnames involved, but it was always owned by descendants of Johann Shenk until it was bought by Ephraim Sechrist in 1920, after it had closed down due to Prohibition. Ownership by the same family had run for 167 years, itself a remarkable achievement. By comparison, the Beams of Kentucky only owned their distillery for about 125 years.

Did Sechrist obtain a license before 1937 in anticipation of reopening the distillery, which he never did? Forman says he bought it from Sechrist in 1942. Since Forman's records say the distillery was licensed as of 1937, but Sechrist never operated it, it is possible that Sechrist was like the distillers in Kentucky. He did some restoration work, including obtaining a federal license to distill, then ran out of money and had to sell. It was a common problem.

Forman's plans for the distillery were themselves interrupted by World War II. He was drafted.

Although Forman was relatively old at 34, all men ages 21 to 45 were eligible for service during WWII.

Due to his uncertain future, and with the liquor brokerage his primary business interest, Forman sold the Schaefferstown distillery to a company called Logansport, which was subsequently absorbed by Schenley, one of the post-Prohibition liquor industry giants.

Schenley's part of the story is next. Lou Forman will be back.

6. The Cincinnati Connection.

One of the most significant figures in the post-Prohibition distilled spirits business was Lewis Rosenstiel.

Born in Cincinnati in 1891, Rosenstiel belonged to one of the first families of the Queen City's Jewish community. He was a grandson of Frederick A. Johnson, the first Jewish child born in that city.

The family had many business interests, including distilled spirits. Rosenstiel's uncle was an executive at the Susquemec Distilling Co. in Milton, Kentucky, south of Cincinnati on the Ohio River. Rosenstiel went to work there as a teenager. By 1914 he was on the company's board of directors. By 1918, at age 27, he was running the place.

Susquemec began as the Snyder Distillery in 1840 and was run by the Snyder family until it was destroyed by fire in 1879. Rebuilt the next year, it was renamed Susquemec and run by James Levy & Brothers, Cincinnati whiskey wholesalers. Rosenstiel's family took it over in about 1910.

Distilleries being taken over by their customers was nothing new. Distilleries always had financing problems. Selling out to their best customer was a common solution. In most cases, the former owner stayed on as an employee and very little changed.

After Prohibition closed Susquemec and every other distillery in the country, the 30-year-old Rosenstiel and some of his associates formed a company called Cincinnati Distributing Corp. to sell medicinal whiskey. To obtain their license they bought an old Pennsylvania distillery that already had one. It gave Rosenstiel's company a new name: Schenley.

The Schenley Distillery was in the town of Schenley, which is in Western Pennsylvania near Pittsburgh. The town and its distillery aren't part of this story. They didn't play a big role in the Schenley company either. To Rosenstiel, it was just a name, a name attached to an all-important medicinal spirits license. The renamed company stayed in Cincinnati.

Buying distilleries and their whiskey stocks throughout Prohibition positioned Rosenstiel and company to dominate the industry when it became legal again in December of 1933. They didn't keep Susquemec, which never reopened, but did buy two distilleries in Lawrenceburg, Indiana, just west of Cincinnati, and merged them under the name Old Quaker. There were four big distilled spirits producers in the country after Repeal. Lew Rosenstiel's Schenley was the biggest.

By 1937, Schenley had outgrown Cincinnati and moved the company's headquarters into the Empire State Building in New York. It was still the old Cincinnati crew, including several members of the Jacobi family. Schenley, largest of the 'big four' post-Prohibition liquor producers, would come to control about 25 percent of the United States distilled spirits market. The other big companies were National Distillers, Hiram Walker, and Seagram's.

Schenley was a major player for more than 50 years. In 1987, a shadow of its former self, it was acquired by Guinness, making it part of what is now Diageo. Today, Diageo dominates the distilled spirits industry much as Schenley did a half-century ago.

Rosentiel died in 1975. There is a lot more to his story, but it doesn't concern us. His ex-wife insisted that he used to play dress up with J. Edgar Hoover. Notorious Cold War lawyer Roy Cohn was disbarred for trying to change Rosentiel's will on Rosentiel's death bed. There have been allegations that Rosentiel was involved with organized crime both during and after Prohibition. It's wild stuff, but has nothing to do with our story. Too bad.

Rosentiel's significance to our story is that he thought very highly of a young man named Adolph H. Hirsch.

Although not as ruinous as Prohibition, the onset of World War II was another major setback for the American whiskey industry. During the war, many distilleries ceased or curtailed whiskey production to make neutral alcohol for munitions and other military uses. If they made whiskey at all, they sold most of it to the military as medicinal whiskey for the troops.

Only when there was surplus grain and surplus distilling capacity were distilleries permitted to make whiskey for civilian sale and consumption.

Making whiskey and neutral alcohol for the war effort was both patriotic and profitable. Nobody ever goes broke doing business with the government during wartime.

During the war, Schenley bought many distilleries, including the one in Schaefferstown, which it bought from Logansport, the company that bought it from Lou Forman.

One of the owners of Logansport was a former and future Schenley executive named Hirsch.

Schenley owned the distillery in Schaefferstown for only a few years but Schenley or people associated with it would continue to be part of this story to the end.

Most significant among them is the legendary whiskey's namesake, Adolph Hirsch.

7. A. H. Hirsch, The Man.

Mannheim is a city in southwest Germany on the Rhine River. Adolph H. Hirsch was born there on June 5, 1908. At the age of 17 he migrated to the United States, where he took a job with A. G. Becker, a prominent investment bank in Chicago. He worked there until 1934, when at the age of 26 he became vice-president of the Bernheim Distillery in Louisville.

As we have already seen, distilleries always need financing, so bankers running distilleries is not unusual. Who better to figure out the long-term financing puzzle? One of the first was Edmund Haynes Taylor Junior (1830-1923), who once owned the distillery now known as Buffalo Trace, as well as many others in and around Frankfort, Kentucky.

The distillery in Louisville, Kentucky, where Hirsch turned from banking to making whiskey, was named for the Bernheim brothers, who created the popular I. W. Harper bourbon brand in 1897. Although they began as wholesalers they eventually built a distillery in Shively that operated until Prohibition.

I. W. Harper Bourbon is still sold by Diageo in Japan and other places, but not in the United States.

The Bernheim company had a medicinal whiskey license and barely stayed in business during Prohibition selling medicinal spirits. Before Prohibition ended, two Chicago-based whiskey merchants named Emil Schwarzhaupt and Leo Gerngross acquired all of the company's assets except the property in Shively. Instead, they acquired a distillery on the west side of Louisville, renamed it Bernheim, and began to make I. W. Harper Bourbon there as soon as Prohibition ended. That distillery, located on West Breckinridge Street at Seventeenth Street, is where Hirsch went to work in 1934.

Though it was rebuilt in 1992, the distillery is still there. It is owned by Heaven Hill. Except for the distillery, most of the buildings on the property are from Hirsch's time.

There is no direct evidence of this, but it seems likely that the Becker firm provided financing for Schwarzhaupt and Gerngross, and that is how they became acquainted with young Mr. Hirsch. There may also have been a family or old-world connection, as there often was. We don't know. It is known that the three men remained close for the rest of their lives. It is not known if Hirsch had an ownership stake in Bernheim, but that seems likely.

Three years after Hirsch joined them, Schwarzhaupt and Gerngross followed another familiar pattern of the post-Prohibition period. They sold the Bernheim Distillery to Lewis Rosenstiel's booming Schenley Products Company, which had just moved its offices from Cincinnati to New York City.

The two older men, Schwarzhaupt and Gerngross, took their money and moved on, but Hirsch remained in Louisville under the Schenley regime until he was transferred to New York to run Bernheim from there. Bernheim was a company division, responsible for the manufacturing, sales, and marketing of I. W. Harper bourbon and other brands made at the Louisville distillery.

Hirsch left Schenley in December, 1941 (age 33), just as the U.S. entered World War II. Soon the American distilled spirits industry would be gearing up to produce industrial alcohol for the war effort. Alcohol was used to make everything from munitions to synthetic rubber. At first, the War Department believed the sugar cane distilleries in Texas, Louisiana, and other Gulf states would be sufficient. When they realized the coastal plants would need to add capacity, and were vulnerable to attack, inland whiskey-makers were pressed into service.

Although large distilleries were required to switch, small ones could continue to make whiskey. Adolph Hirsch immediately recognized the business opportunity. He, one Samuel Glass, and a third partner acquired Pennsylvania Distilling Company, which already owned two small, rural distilleries in Pennsylvania. They renamed the company Logansport and acquired a third distillery, the one in Schaefferstown that they bought from Louis Forman.

Although we don't know if the distillery in Schaefferstown operated at all between 1933 and 1942, we know it was running by at least 1942. Logansport ran all three distilleries for the duration of the war. They primarily made bourbon whiskey. We don't know if their bourbon went to the services for medical use, or if some or all of it went into the civilian marketplace.

When the war ended, Hirsch and his partners sold Logansport to Schenley and Hirsch rejoined Schenley for about four months, after which he announced his retirement to "pursue charitable activity." He was just 38 and, as it would turn out, far from finished with the whiskey business.

In 1956, Hirsch un-retired and moved back to New York to rejoin Schenley for a third time, this time as Executive Vice President, one of the highest positions in the company. The next year, the Schaefferstown distillery was acquired by Hirsch's former partner in Logansport, Samuel Glass, who renamed it Pennco.

Hirsch really had pursued charitable activity during his first retirement. In returning to Schenley, he did not discontinue those activities. In 1958, he succeeded Leo Gerngross as president of the Emil Schwarzhaupt Foundation, a position he held until at least 1979. The Schwarzhaupt Foundation funded programs to promote American citizenship, "especially among the foreign-born," and to that end made major grants to the University of Chicago and other institutions.

In July, 1960, Hirsch retired from Schenley for good, at age 52.

We do not know very much about his activities thereafter, but he apparently kept his hand in the whiskey business. Dick Stoll, a key player whose account will be along shortly, and who knew Hirsch after 1955, described him as, "a whiskey broker, like Lou Forman.

8. Louis Forman Returns.

Lou Forman survived the war and returned to his Philadelphia liquor brokerage business. He never forgot about that little distillery near Schaefferstown that he had briefly owned before the conflict. He still had the itch to own it and in his mind it made even more business sense now than it had before, because all over the country brokers like him were securing their whiskey supply by buying distilleries instead of relying entirely on the shrinking and increasingly volatile bulk whiskey market.

According to Forman's records, he regained control of the distillery in 1950. One might interpret that to mean he bought the place, but he probably didn't.

To run it, Forman hired Charles Everett Beam, a great-great grandson of Johannes Jacob Boehm, a German immigrant whose family lived in Pennsylvania and Maryland before relocating to Kentucky in about 1788. There he began a whiskey-making dynasty. By then he was spelling his name "Beam." All of Kentucky's whiskey-making Beams are descended from him.

Charles Everett Beam brought the family name back to Pennsylvania in 1951 when he began to distill whiskey at the distillery near Schaefferstown. He was 44 and had already run distilleries in Kentucky and several other states.

Charles Everett Beam's father was Joseph L. Beam. He was a revered figure in his hometown of Bardstown, Kentucky, known as 'Mr. Joe,' or 'Pop.' During Prohibition, Pop Beam had briefly been the town's jailer, an elected position. Charles Everett's mother, Katherine McGill, known as 'Ma Beam,' was a formidable person in her own right. She too was from a family of whiskey makers. Her brother, Will McGill, worked with her husband at several different distilleries and after Prohibition became Master Distiller at the Van Winkle family's new Stitzel-Weller Distillery, where his brother-in-law helped out and many of his nephews were employed. Ma Beam was the family 'fixer' who both dominated her sons and smoothed the way for them, long after they became adults.

All of Charles Everett's brothers – all six of them – were distillers.

Pop Beams's first cousin and occasional business partner was James Beauregard Beam, better known as Jim, who had his own distillery that he ran with his brother and their sons. It was and still is a big family. Many Beams live in Nelson County, in and around the cities of Bardstown and New Haven. Charles Everett's daughter, Mary, a major source for this book, lives in Lexington. Many members of the family live in and around Louisville, the state's largest city. The Beam Family Reunion, sponsored by Beam Inc. and held in

September at the Jim Beam Distillery in Clermont, is a huge annual event. All descendants of Jacob Beam are welcome.

It was common, at least in Charles Everett's branch of the Beam family, to be known by your middle name. Charles Everett Beam was generally called Everett. Lou Forman called him Ev.

While renovating the Schaefferstown property, Forman and Beam discovered some of Bomberger's old records in an attic. When they realized the full extent of the distillery's heritage, they decided that was the way to take the business. It was then that Forman coined the name Michter's, which sounded vaguely Pennsylvania Dutch but was actually formed from the first names of his two sons, Michael and Peter.

Forman had big plans for the place, most of which didn't pan out. His records say that he and Beam "decided to cultivate a premium niche market by making old-fashioned pot-still mash whiskey. This traditional method could not be adapted to mass production."

That may, as the records say, have been what they decided to do, but did they follow through? 'Old-fashioned pot-still whiskey' became the distillery's hallmark, a claim that would later be made for A. H. Hirsch Reserve Straight Bourbon Whiskey. We now know it wasn't true. Forman and Beam also planned to package their whiskey in old-fashioned white china crocks, which they did.

Much of the information we have about Forman's role in this story comes from the Hagley Museum collection that is mentioned at the end of Chapter 4. It begins with an official narrative that is essentially

Forman's version of the Michter's tale. As we will see with the "old-fashioned pot-still" claim and many other statements associated with Forman, one must always read his words very carefully. Throughout the record there is a pattern of obfuscation that always stops just short of outright lying. For example, the narrative never claims he owned the distillery in the fifties. It says that he "regained control" of it in 1950 and "lost full control" to Pennco in 1957. The evidence suggests that he did not own it but ostensibly controlled it contractually.

Ever since the late 19th century, whiskey merchants (such as brokers like Forman) have gained control of distilleries without buying them through exclusive sales contracts, in which the distillery agrees to sell all of its production to a particular wholesaler who in turn agrees to buy however much the distillery is able to produce. According to the terms of the contract, the distillery may not sell its whiskey to anyone else and the wholesaler is obliged to buy all of the distillery's output. This is, for example, how the George Dickel Company, a whiskey dealer in Nashville, controlled the Cascade Hollow Distillery in Tullahoma, Tennessee, before Prohibition.

To put a point on it, Forman's letterhead in the fifties identifies his company as, "Louis Forman & Company, brokers of whiskey in bond, distillery controllers."

Forman blamed a nationwide economic recession and consequent whiskey glut for his 1957 loss of control to Pennco.

Regardless of how the ownership change went down, it brought a familiar name back into the picture,

Samuel Glass, Pennco's founder and president. This would mark the second time Glass had helped Forman by buying the foundering Schaefferstown distillery. Glass and Adolph Hirsch had been partners in Logansport, which bought the Schaefferstown distillery from Forman in 1942. With Hirsch on his way back to New York to rejoin Schenley, Glass thought he could again make a business out of Schaefferstown.

Perhaps he figured that, in a few years, his friend Adolph would arrange for Schenley to buy it again and make Glass a nice profit, just like before.

Forman retained ownership of the whiskey he and Beam made between 1951 and 1957, most of which was still aging in the distillery's warehouses. He also retained ownership of the Michter's name, which he began to use to market that whiskey. As planned, he packaged it in old-fashioned white china crocks.

If Forman controlled but did not own the distillery between 1949 and 1957, who did? Schenley? Apparently not.

Although Forman's records are more complete that Fowler's, he neglects to mention Kirk Foulke, who two different sources say owned the distillery right before Pennco. A 1957 letter from Forman to Foulke, on the letterhead of Forman's Philadelphia whiskey brokerage, supports that conclusion. The letter memorializes a verbal agreement between Forman and Foulke to end their business relationship and forgive any claims one might have against the other. In it, Forman refers to, "whiskies produced for my account at the Kirks Pure Rye Distillery Company under our various agreements."

Presumably, Schenley sold it to Foulke in 1950 or 51.

Regardless of who owned it when, Everett Beam was always there as master distiller. Under Pennco, the distillery mostly did contract distilling for large liquor companies. They would make bourbon, rye; whatever the customer wanted. Forman, with his Michter's whiskey, continued to be a customer, although he also bought and sold whiskey from other distilleries. He was, after all, still a whiskey broker.

Under the leadership of Samuel Glass, the distillery did relatively well through the rest of the 1950s and into the 1960s. An article from the Lebanon Press and Journal of Lebanon, Pennsylvania, dated May 12, 1966, describes the distillery in its heyday. The article says it was relatively small as modern distilleries went, with a daily capacity of 750 bushels of grain, yielding 60 barrels of whiskey a day. It had warehouse space for about 60,000 barrels, which suggests they were dumping about 15,000 barrels a year.

Although it was the smallest distillery in Pennsylvania at the time, there were comparably-sized whiskey distilleries in Kentucky, Illinois, and other states during that period.

As a contract distiller, Pennco prided itself on making a high quality product. After his retirement, Everett Beam was quoted (in an article in the Lebanon newspaper) as saying that many of the best known brands of Pennsylvania rye whiskey, owned and marketed by large corporations such as Schenley and Continental, were actually made by him at Pennco.

He was also very proud of his original formula for the Michter's Original Sour Mash Whiskey Pennco continued to make and Lou Forman continued to sell.

After a good run of more than a decade, Pennco began to struggle when the distilled spirits market changed drastically in the late 1960s. Like most American whiskey distilleries, Pennco saw its sales decline dramatically. In about 1975, the company failed and went into receivership.

Forman then formed a corporation called Michter's Distillery Inc., with a group of Lebanon county businessmen, and bought the distillery at the foreclosure sale.

We now know that the Hirsch bourbon was made in February-March of 1974, so it was already in the warehouses when the company failed. More details on that to come, but let's finish with the distillery.

In 1976, the distillery resumed operations as Michter's. In 1977, the company produced a business plan, probably as part of an effort to secure additional financing. It indicated seven "separate, but related, lines of business." They were: (1) wholesale case goods, (2) retail case goods, (3) contract distilling, (4) storage and handling (5) admissions and other related tourism activities (6) dried grain and (7) export.

The only new thing on the list, from what Pennco had done, was number five, "admissions and other related tourism activities." To that end, the place was spruced up and a major new attraction was added, a complete pot still distillery capable of producing about one barrel of spirit per day, which was unveiled as part of the American Bicentennial celebration in 1976.

We'll talk more about that small distillery later but note the ratio. The big distillery filled 60 barrels a day. The small distillery could fill one.

We now pick up the story from newspaper clippings, most of which were collected by Yvonne Fowler and posted on her Michter's web site.

A 1979 Associated Press (AP) story reported Michter's sale to "Theodore B. Veru of Fort Lee, New Jersey...a former executive with Schenley Distillers."

His prior association with Schenley notwithstanding, Ted Veru is best known as Co-Chairman and Co-CEO of Lois/USA Inc., a major international advertising agency. The other "Co-" was the agency's legendary namesake, George Lois, one of the most successful advertising art directors of the 'Mad Men' era. Lois was best known for 92 iconic covers he created for Esquire Magazine between 1962 and 1972.

Michter's wasn't particularly successful under Veru, but it had good advertising. Veru was just one in a long line of brief, unsuccessful owners of Michter's during the 70s and 80s. Although we have no definitive evidence, the sale to Veru seems to have marked the end of the line for Lou Forman, who was 71-years-old and probably tired of beating his head against the wall with a business that never quite seemed either to fail or succeed.

In 1980, the Michter's Distillery became a National Historic Landmark. Tourism had become a big part of its business. Michter's was attracting 55,000 visitors a year. Forman's 1977 business plan had predicted 75,000 by 1983.

Admission fees and gift shop sales were supporting the distillery.

In 1985, The Daily News of Lebanon, Pennsylvania, ran a light piece about a new Michter's decanter being introduced. All it said about ownership was that "the distillery has been through several owners." At this and similar events, members of the Bomberger family were trotted out for their historical connection. Although they had no other role at the company, they were considered the keepers of its heritage. Yvonne Fowler continued to fulfill that role after the distillery's demise, by maintaining a web site among other efforts.

According to a March, 1989 newspaper article, Michter's filed for Chapter 11 protection in 1980, after its bank foreclosed, but was still operating nine years later, running its stills for about four months a year. During production season they filled about 50 barrels a day. They were running at less than one-third capacity.

Other clippings say the bankruptcy filing came in 1989, shortly before the distillery stopped production. There may have been several such events.

All sources agree that Michter's stopped production in late 1989 or early 1990. In its last year, it sold a mere 10,000 cases of its signature Michter's Original Sour Mash Whiskey.

Things went downhill quickly after that.

By 1991, according to newspaper reports at the time, the distillery was not just closed, the company and property had been abandoned. No one could find the last owners, a company called Aquari Holding Company (spelled 'Aquarii' in some accounts). Although there were still allegedly 300,000 gallons of whiskey in the warehouses, there was a big, overdue property tax bill looming. That's why the owners skipped. The county then seized the property for the unpaid taxes.

All of this was reported in the local newspaper. The news prompting the story was that thieves were breaking into the warehouses and stealing whiskey. Since no owners could be found, the county police had tried to secure the property.

Typically when distilleries stop producing, they either sell their aging stock or keep a rump operation in place to continue bottling and selling the product until it's all gone. In this case, the owners abandoned the entire operation. The liabilities were too great and the prospects too slim. One day the distillery's workers were putting newly-filled barrels into the racks. The next day everyone was gone, the lights were off, and the gates were chained shut.

By 1994, the whiskey was gone too, and the land and buildings were sold after a deal was made on the back taxes. Both the new owner and county officials talked about getting the distillery back into operation to "allow it to generate tax revenue once again."

This was probably a pipedream even then. By the mid-nineties there were no more active whiskey distilleries in the eastern United States. The American whiskey industry had contracted into Kentucky and Tennessee, and very few of the remaining distilleries there were operating at anything close to capacity. The micro-distillery movement was still more than a decade in the future.

By 1996, the Michter's property was being liquidated piecemeal. In 1997, with little remaining at the site except a few ruined buildings, the U.S. Interior Department revoked its landmark status. It was, in landmarks lingo, "de-designated." It looked like it was, after 244 years, finally all over.

And so it was, for the distillery at least. The legend of A. H. Hirsch Reserve Straight Bourbon Whiskey was just getting started.

Lou Forman's name does not appear in the record after the sale of Michter's to Veru. All rights to the Michter's name seem to have stayed with the distillery after that. When the business was finally abandoned, so was the trademark. A few years later, someone was clever enough to recognize that the Michter's name, at least, still had value so they simply reregistered it. Through that simple and inexpensive act they were able to claim the entire history of the little distillery outside of Schaefferstown for a completely unrelated company. That's called good business.

Louis Forman died on January 23, 2002, age 93.

9. The Barrel-A-Day Distillery.

Back in 1976, as part of its tourism strategy, Michter's commissioned the Kentucky still maker Vendome to build a small 'barrel-a-day distillery' to demonstrate the whiskey-making process for visitors. Vendome, itself a century-old, family-owned company based in Louisville, makes most of the stills and associated equipment used by American whiskey makers.

The barrel-a-day distillery consisted of two copper pot stills, three cypress fermenters, a mash cooker, and other equipment. It was installed in the original Bomberger Distillery building at Michter's as part of the American Bicentennial celebration.

Billing itself as America's Oldest Distillery, and being in a history-rich part of the state, Michter's naturally received a share of reflected Bicentennial glory.

Living in Louisville at the time was Everett Beam, Michter's retired Master Distiller. He still had a relationship with the company and probably worked with Vendome on the design and fabrication of the model distillery. It may have been small but it was not a prop or a toy. It was intended to be a working distillery that made quality whiskey.

The barrel-a-day distillery was operated in addition to the main, conventional distillery so tourists would have something to see when the conventional distillery was silent, as it was more and more often. A modern American whiskey distillery can only run at one speed. You can slow it down a little, but mainly you control output through shutdowns. By the mid-seventies, Michter's was operating less than half of the year.

The barrel-a-day distillery was installed to pick up the slack, tourist-wise. It ran according to the tourism schedule. Its small scale also made it easier to explain the whiskey distillation process to visitors. It ran five days a week for about eight hours a day, unlike the big distillery which, when it was running, would run 24 hours a day.

Michter's claimed that the barrel-a-day distillery "duplicates the way whiskey was made on the premises prior to 1840." This is another example of Michter's making a marketing claim that had little basis in fact. No effort was made to achieve historical accuracy with the barrel-a-day distillery. Although it was a true pot still distillery it was made with the technology of 1976, not 1840, and so could be operated safely and effectively. It wasn't an authentic 19th century distillery, but it was a real distillery that could make good whiskey.

Since the 1950s, Michter's had claimed to be 'old-fashioned pot still whiskey.' Now, for the first time, they had an actual all-pot-still distillery to show visitors. The stills were alembics, true pot stills, uncommon then and uncommon still in the United States. Most modern micro-distillers claim they use pot stills but their pots have rectification columns on top, making them more of a hybrid, a batch still with rectification capabilities.

When the big distillery was silent, which was most of the time, tourists got to see the aging warehouses, where whiskey was always being withdrawn and dumped, and the bottling hall, which was usually active. They could see the big distillery, which was impressive even when dark. All that plus the barrel-a-day distillery and the gift shop, and it was still a pretty good tour.

By a special act of the Pennsylvania legislature, Michter's was allowed to sell its whiskey at the distillery. All other distilled spirits sales in the state went through the state-controlled liquor system. Toward the end, the distillery was just about the only place that sold Michter's Original Sour Mash Whiskey.

Although it was called 'barrel-a-day' because it could produce about 50 gallons of spirit in an eight-hour day, at least some of that spirit never saw the inside of a barrel. It was sold, as what micro-distillers today call white whiskey, in the gift shop. The rest was barreled and aged, and used in regular production of Michter's Whiskey and other products.

During the 1996 liquidation sale at Michter's, David Beam acquired the barrel-a-day distillery and transported it to Bardstown, Kentucky, where it sat for years on display next to a motel he owned. He never tried to set it up and operate it.

When he bought the distillery, David Beam had just retired as distiller at Jim Beam. He is the younger son of Carl 'Shucks' Beam, and therefore the grandson of Jim Beam's brother, Park. David's brother is Baker Beam, after whom Baker's Bourbon is named. All of them – sons, father and grandfather -- were distillers at the main Jim Beam Distillery in Clermont, Kentucky.

Baker and David Beam grew up in the big, wood frame house that still overlooks the Clermont distillery. Parker Beam, longtime Master Distiller at Heaven Hill, is their first cousin. Booker Noe was a second cousin. Everett Beam was a more distant cousin.

David and Baker literally grew up at the Jim Beam Distillery, and Parker was a frequent guest. The three boys liked to ride their bikes together in Bernheim Forest, which is right across the road from the distillery. Bernheim Forest is a 10,000 acre park and nature preserve, given to the people of Kentucky by Issac Wolfe Bernheim, founder of the company once run by Adolph Hirsch.

The Kentucky-Tennessee whiskey business is a very small world.

David is the last family member with the surname of Beam to have worked as a distiller at the Beam company. That role has since shifted to the Noe family, descendents of Jim Beam's daughter, Margaret, first to her son, Booker Noe Junior, and now to Booker's son, Fred, whose full name is Frederick Booker Noe III.

David Beam has always been ambiguous about why he bought the Michter's barrel-a-day distillery. Some days he says it was just because he had always lived near a distillery and liked to have it around, on other days he said it was so his three boys could start a small distillery if they wanted to and reclaim their heritage. Whenever any of them showed any interest in doing just that, he said they would be crazy to attempt it and proceeded to talk them out of it.

Troy, the oldest, was never much interested. Bill, the middle son, had accompanied his father on the trips to Pennsylvania and urged him to buy the equipment. John Ed, the youngest, got interested as he got older.

Remember the Michter's barrel-a-day distillery. We're not finished with it yet.

10. The Whiskey Itself.

Back in 1990, when Michter's closed and was abandoned, and Lebanon County officials were busy trying to deter whiskey thieves, those officials claimed that about 300,000 gallons of whiskey, in barrels, remained in the warehouses.

Was *that* the whiskey that became A. H. Hirsch Reserve, rescued by Hirsch in those dark days, as some believe?

No.

There is very little we can say for certain about the whiskey that was still in the warehouses at Michter's after 1990 except this. (1) There was a considerable amount of whiskey there (way more than 300,000 gallons), (2) most of it was made to be sold as Michter's Original Sour Mash Whiskey, and (3) nobody wanted it.

Everyone who controlled Michter's up to the end and *after* the end – the final owners, the bank, the county government – they were all looking for money and would have sold anything there that anyone was willing to buy, including every drop of whiskey in every barrel remaining in the distillery's warehouses. They would have sold it cheap, as evidenced by the fact that they eventually gave it away (probably). Yet there it sat. To Lebanon County it was what the law calls an attractive nuisance, tempting thieves and thereby inconveniencing law enforcement.

Some of those who attempted to steal whiskey from the warehouses were local teenagers, and a few were injured in the process. It was a big problem for local officials.

There are complications in selling a distilled spirit that don't burden the sale of machines, tanks, lumber or real estate. The buyer has to have the proper license. But plenty of people had that license and no doubt were aware of the whiskey's availability. Merely disposing of an alcohol and water solution that is about 65 percent alcohol is problematic. You can't just dump it into the sewers, not legally at least.

We can assume that a large percentage of the whiskey that remained at Michter's after it closed was still immature, most likely distilled in the last several years of operations. The rest would have been older whiskey or other spirits (e.g., raisin brandy). It's possible some or all of it was flawed in some way. Any of those reasons might explain why, for the desperate entities that controlled the distillery up to and beyond its final collapse, no offering price was low enough to find a buyer.

We know of three other factors that contributed to the whiskey's undesirability.

First, the bulk whiskey market was incredibly depressed. Second, the mash bill for Michter's Original Sour Mash Whiskey was 50 percent corn, 38 percent rye and 12 percent malted barley. Named types, such as bourbon and rye, have to be at least 51 percent corn or rye, respectively. Therefore, Michter's could not be sold as either bourbon or rye. It could be sold as 'whiskey,' with no modifiers, or as 'Pennsylvania whiskey,' but Michter's collapse proved that the consumer market for 'Pennsylvania whiskey' had pretty much dried up.

Generic whiskey, packaged and sold at retail, is a 'bottom shelf' product, with a razor-thin profit margin. In those years of the great whiskey glut, well-made and well-aged bourbon from major producers was being sold as generic whiskey, there was so much excess whiskey around. There was no reason to take a chance on some questionable spirit from an abandoned distillery with no one to vouch for it.

The other problem was that some percentage of it was being aged in used barrels. The whiskey aged in *new* barrels could be called 'straight whiskey' if it was at least two years old. The whiskey aged in *used* barrels could not. Again, it could only be sold as whiskey. Considering all of these factors and perhaps others still unknown, nobody was willing to take a chance on that whiskey at any price.

So what *did* happen to it? It was *not* flushed down the sewers, as one rumor had it. The answer is coming. For now suffice it to say it did *not* become A. H. Hirsch Reserve.

But if *that* whiskey wasn't the whiskey that became A. H. Hirsch Reserve Straight Bourbon Whiskey, then what was?

Because of the 'old-fashioned pot still' claim, some people have speculated that A. H. Hirsch Reserve was whiskey made in the Michter's barrel-a-day distillery. We now know that's impossible. Simple math could have told us that if we had thought about it. The first A.

H. Hirsch Reserve appeared in late 1989 as a 15-year-old. That means it had to have been distilled in 1974 or earlier, two years before the barrel-a-day distillery arrived.

Here is what we know about the whiskey that became A. H. Hirsch Reserve.

It was made in a single batch of 400 barrels. That's about an eight-day run in the big distillery at Michter's. A standard whiskey barrel holds 53 gallons. The Hirsch whiskey was legally bourbon, not Michter's Original Sour Mash. The distillery in Schaefferstown had always made bourbon and rye, both for its own portfolio and as part of its contract distilling business.

Early versions of the Hirsch story said that Adolph Hirsch acquired his bourbon in 1989, just before Michter's ceased operations. We now know that Hirsch *commissioned* the whiskey in 1974, as a contract distilling job. Hirsch, like Forman, was a customer for Pennco's contract distilling, storage, and handling services. Hirsch may have entered into many such contracts with Pennco and other distilleries over the years. This one was unique, though not in the way you may think.

11. The Label.

In the late 1990s, Preiss Imports acquired A. H. Hirsch Reserve from the Hue family. At that point, Gordon Hue and his family had been marketing the whiskey for almost ten years and most of it was still unsold. It had been removed from wood to prevent it from over-aging and was languishing in stainless steel tanks, itself an expense and risk. All of it was at least 16-years-old. In 2003, Preiss had it all bottled at the Buffalo Trace Distillery in Frankfort, Kentucky.

If you have or have ever seen a bottle of A. H. Hirsch Reserve Straight Bourbon Whiskey, it probably is from that final run. There were more bottles produced in that run than in all of the previous releases combined. The story its packaging tells is important, therefore, because that story is the 'official' one, and the only story most people who bought or sold the whiskey ever knew.

The simple but elegant, soft-shouldered clear glass bottle is topped with a gold foil capsule. At the capsule's base there is a burgundy band. An inscription on the band, in gold, reads, 'America's First 5-Star Bourbon.'

The front label, from top to bottom, reads: 16 Years Old. Distilled in the Spring of 1974. A. H. Hirsch

Reserve Straight Bourbon Whiskey. Pot-Stilled Sour Mash. Bottled by Hirsch Distillers, Frankfort, Kentucky. 45.8% ALC/VOL (91.6° proof). 750 ML.

The back label copy is long. Headlined "A Masterwork," it tells the whiskey's story as it had been passed down from the previous owners, with perhaps a few original embellishments. These are the principal claims you see whenever A. H. Hirsch Reserve is discussed. They were repeated in Preiss Imports promotional materials. Preiss bought the story, in at least two senses of that word, when he bought the brand.

It goes like this:

"This extraordinary bourbon had a long, dramatic journey from its inception to your glass. In fact, the history behind A. H. Hirsch Reserve speaks volumes about why it is not just the finest American bourbon ever made, but indeed a rare national artifact.

"The sublime, amber-colored whiskey in this bottle was distilled in 1974 in the small copper pot-stills of Michter's Distillery. Nestled in the heart of Pennsylvania, the distillery originated in the mid-1700s when Kentucky was just a twinkle in Daniel Boone's eye. It is quite justifiably listed as a National Historic Landmark.

"The combination of an arduous distilling process, an unusual recipe including rye, and 16 years of peaceful slumber in the wood are partly why Hirsch Reserve is such a magnificent spirit. The rest must be put down to the sheer force of history and, perhaps, a touch of magic.

"In 1989, the last remaining barrels were brought to Kentucky for final aging and bottling – this whiskey was awarded America's first five-star rating. Simply stated, there is no other bourbon on any shelf that compares with its bouquet, flavor, depth and overall complexity.

"A. H. Hirsch Reserve whiskey is an evocation of a specific time and place. We present it here for your discerning taste and lasting enjoyment."

Let's dissect that label copy based on what we now know. Advertising hyperbole aside, here are the statements we know are not true.

- A. H. Hirsch Reserve bourbon was *not* made in "small copper pot stills."
- There was nothing particularly "arduous" about the process by which it was made. It was made the same way all bourbon whiskey was made at the time.
- Its recipe was in no way "unusual." Rye grain is an ingredient in most bourbon recipes.
- When this label was printed, Michter's Distillery was no longer a National Historic Landmark.

Although there are still a few things we don't know, in particular about *why* the whiskey was made, we now know just about everything about *how* it was made. That's because we asked the person who made it.

12. Dick Stoll's Perspective.

For all of the interest in A. H. Hirsch Reserve bourbon in the 1990s and thereafter, all of the speculation about its origins, and all of the words written about it, nobody thought to ask the distiller who made it until I did in 2009. As I write this in 2012, Dick Stoll, master distiller at Pennco/Michter's from 1972 until 1990, is alive and well, and still living in Lebanon, Pennsylvania.

Many thanks to the friends who told me about Mr. Stoll and helped me contact him.

According to Stoll, he went to work at the distillery in Schaefferstown in 1955 and stayed there until it closed on, according to him, February 14, 1990. He remembers the exact date because he was running the place at the time, on behalf of the bank that owned it through default. On that day the bank called and told him to send everybody home and shut the place down.

When it finally closed, Dick Stoll had worked at the little distillery in Schaefferstown for 35 years.

Stoll recalls that when he went to work there in 1955, the distillery was owned by a man named Kirk Foulke and called Kirk's Pure Rye Distillery. Foulke had bought it, presumably from Schenley, in 1949 and made whiskey there continuously until 1952. The stills were silent between 1952 and 1955. Then the distillery was sold to Pennco. There was still some of Kirk's whiskey in the warehouses, and that kept Pennco going as a business after they started to make whiskey again, until their own whiskey came of age.

Stoll was not a distiller at first. He didn't have a background in it like Everett Beam. He was just a hand, doing whatever jobs around the distillery needed to be done. He learned from Beam and eventually took over when Beam retired.

The distillery in Schaefferstown was a big part of Dick Stoll's life. He even met his wife there. She was a local teacher who brought groups of children through for tours.

Stoll insists that Louis Forman never owned the distillery in the 1950s. Stoll didn't arrive until 1955, and Forman's records are ambiguous. They talk about Forman 'controlling' the distillery during those years, not owning it. As should be apparent by now, who actually owned the distillery wasn't always clear. Sometimes it may have seemed like its major customers were its owners and, in a way, they were. This is because of a peculiarity in the way American distilleries have long operated.

American whiskey distilleries have a long history of operating under assumed business names. You may also see this referred to as a "dba," which stands for "doing business as." Assumed business names are permitted but they have to be registered so the government and, by extension, the public can determine who the 'real' owner is. You can use an assumed business name for any legal purpose, but you can't use it to hide your true identity.

It was customary before Prohibition for a distillery to be legally 'rented' for some period of time, during which it made whiskey for a third party, and during that period it was, in legal fact, that party's distillery. The distiller was the same guy, all of the hands were the same, it was the same equipment, the same raw materials, and the same recipes. Everything was the same except the customer's name, which for that time was also the distillery's name.

Not every distillery was in what we would now call the contract distilling business, but those that were would have a box full of small signs – they called them shingles – each bearing a different distillery name. Often they were brand names. Sometimes they were the names of defunct distilleries. In either case, the name was owned by the distillery's customer. On days when the distillery was making spirit for that customer to be sold as Old Such & Such Whiskey, the sign above the door said 'Old Such & Such Distillery.' While that shingle was up, it legally was the Old Such & Such Distillery. There was supporting paperwork too, of course. It was all part of the transaction.

Many aspects of this custom persisted into the modern era and some continue to this day. That's why there may be a hundred different brands of American whiskey on the shelf, but it all comes from the same dozen or so major distilleries. Knob Creek, for example is made by Beam Inc. at the Jim Beam Distillery, but the name 'Beam' appears nowhere on the label. Instead it says, "Distilled and Bottled by Knob Creek Distillery, Clermont, Kentucky." 'Knob

Creek Distillery' is an assumed business name. Knob Creek Distillery does not exist except on paper.

Another example can be found within our story. If you recall the label from the previous chapter, "Hirsch Distillers, Frankfort, Kentucky," was an assumed business name for Buffalo Trace Distillery. The name was registered with the Kentucky Secretary of State so Buffalo Trace could bottle that last batch of A. H. Hirsch Reserve on behalf of Preiss Imports.

Another term for an assumed business name, or dba, is a fictitious business name. That's what Pennsylvania calls them. As a contract distiller, Pennco had plenty of them. Until 1975, when it became the distillery's actual name, Michter's was one of its fictitious business names.

Assumed or fictitious business names are not unique to the whiskey trade, many businesses use them. Chevrolet, Buick, and Cadillac, for example, are brand names but also assumed business names used by General Motors Corporation. Hotpoint is an assumed business name of General Electric.

Because companies are required by law to register their dba names, today it's usually easy to find out who the *actual* producer of a particular whiskey is by looking up the dba name in the Kentucky Secretary of State's database.

Just like a distillery might have many names, those names might have several homes. Over time, any number of different distilleries may have briefly served as the 'Old Such & Such Distillery.' Although everyone has always said A. H. Hirsch was distilled at Michter's in 1974, the distillery was Pennco then.

'Michter's Distillery' was one of the fictitious business names Pennco used, though not for the Hirsch job.

As we learned in Chapter 7, Samuel Glass and Adolph Hirsch were partners in Logansport, the company that purchased the Schaefferstown distillery from Forman in 1942 and ran it during the war. There is no evidence that Hirsch was involved with Glass's Pennco, except as a customer like Forman. It was in that capacity that he commissioned the 400 barrels of bourbon that would eventually be bottled under his name.

We have no information about who owned Pennco besides Samuel Glass, if anyone did. Forman often *acted* like the owner, but was not. The best evidence we have says Kirk Foulke owned it pre-1957. Everett Beam was very close to Forman. Was he Forman's employee or Foulke's? His family just knows he worked for the distillery.

In his *World Guide to Whisky,* first published in 1987, Michael Jackson waxed nostalgically about Kirk's Rye, which he referred to as a "much-loved product" of the distillery, "named after one of its owners."

Because of a lawsuit in which he was involved, we know Kirk Foulke owned a farm in the same township, which he sold in 1959. The sale included farm equipment, a large number of pigs, and a garbage disposal contract with the City of Reading.

Stoll says it was Forman who got the distillery landmarked. No one disputes that Forman came up with the name Michter's.

But it was Samuel Glass's Pennco that owned the place from 1957 until 1975, not Lou Forman's Michter's. It was Pennco, not Michter's, that received the contract from Adolph Hirsch in 1974 to make the 400 barrels of bourbon that became A. H. Hirsch Reserve.

Pennco was never a brand, however, so it's possible that for some or all of that period, the distillery was popularly known as Michter's to promote Lou Forman's Michter's brand, which was indeed made there. Even though the distillery and the brand were owned by two different entities, it was a symbiotic relationship. Forman always had a business interest if not an ownership stake and for some or all of the period when Foulke owned it, Forman may have controlled it contractually.

According to Stoll, Kirk Foulke got stock in Pennco in return for the whiskey still in the warehouses. Pennco also brought whiskey in from Continental in Philadelphia. Throughout Pennco's ownership it did extensive business with the much larger Continental, which may have had an ownership stake. As Stoll recalls, Pennco also sold whiskey to Canadian distilleries, and made Baltimore Pure Rye for Brown-Forman.

Michael Jackson mentions that Schaefferstown made Wild Turkey Rye for Austin-Nichols into the 1980s, even after Austin-Nichols acquired the Ripy Distillery in Lawrenceburg, Kentucky. It also made Old Overholt Rye for National Distillers, according to Jackson. Everett Beam implied as much in his post-retirement interviews.

Although most sources, including Beam's daughter, Mary, refer to her father as Everett Beam, he was Charlie to Dick Stoll.

In June of 1972, Stoll recalls, Hurricane Agnes struck. It remains the worst natural disaster in

Pennsylvania history. At Pennco it flooded everything and the company went under financially as a result. As Stoll remembers it, the company failed in 1972, right after the storm. Most other sources put the Pennco failure at 1975, but that doesn't mean it wasn't caused by the 1972 natural disaster.

Also in 1972, Everett Beam retired and moved back to Kentucky, although he continued to have an advisory role with the company and the title of vice president. Undoubtedly, the company wanted to keep him on the payroll so it could talk about the illustrious Beam family. Stoll remembers it as a heart attack but Beam's remaining children say, no, he simply turned 65 and retired. He had heart problems in his later years and a heart attack killed him in 1989.

Forman and some local businessmen bought the distillery at the foreclosure sale in 1975. Forman became president and the distillery officially became Michter's.

Regardless of when the ownership changed, the distillery was struggling. It tried different businesses. It made raisin brandy, using raisins imported from Turkey, to sell to companies that made fortified wines such as sherry and port. Hiram Walker put a cordials plant in. Anything to make a buck.

Stoll stayed on in Schaefferstown after Beam left and became Master Distiller. He continued to use Everett Beam's recipes and methods. He was supervised by long-time plant manager George Shattls.

During the 1970s, Forman and his local businessmen partners pushed hard to develop tourism at Michter's. Tourism was good both for the distillery and for other local businesses the group's members owned. With the claim that Michter's was the oldest operating distillery in America, they made a big push for tourism in 1976, the American Bicentennial year.

According to Stoll, Forman and company always intended to build the distillery up and resell it. At one point, Austin-Nichols wanted to buy it to make Wild Turkey Rye there. (They had purchased the Kentucky distillery to make their bourbon in 1971.) Instead, Ted Veru came in. Veru, you'll recall, was a former Schenley manager and acclaimed Madison Avenue advertising executive.

Veru promised to make them more money than the sale to Austin-Nichols would bring, but he didn't. They got heavily into the business of selling collectible decanters which, of course, came filled with Michter's Original Sour Mash Whiskey. This business did well for a time. Veru even bought a ceramics plant in Ohio. According to Stoll, Veru ran all of the money out of Michter's, then got himself out, sometime in the early 1980s.

Through all of the twists and turns of the later years, Dick Stoll stayed at Michter's. Commonwealth National Bank, of Harrisburg, Pennsylvania, took it over but had another company manage it for them. The distillery still mashed about 300 bushels a day when it was operating. When the main distillery was silent they ran the barrel-a-day distillery for the tourists. The bank tried to sell it but a deal never went through. They were supposed to get a bond on the whiskey but never did.

On February 14, 1990, Valentine's Day, the love ran out. The bank called Stoll and told him to send everyone home and shut it down.

Dick Stoll recalls some crazy times toward the end. At one point they had some moldy malt, but his bosses told him to use it anyway. Moldy grain makes moldy-tasting whiskey. They sold it to a Korean outfit.

Going into old stock, they bottled a 20-year-old rye for Fuji in Japan. The Japanese interest in extra aged American whiskey was just beginning in the late 1980s. There was some of the rye left in the tank after Fuji's order was completed. The bosses had them bottle it and sold it, for $20 a bottle, as Michter's Rye.

Stoll remembers the Hirsch bourbon. He confirms that Adolph Hirsch owned it, but he didn't buy it when it was 15-years-old. He bought it before it was made, contracted for it, 400 barrels of bourbon, about 8 days of production. It was made by Stoll and his crew in the late winter of 1974. Hirsch was still in the business then as a broker, like Lou Forman had been.

It was, as Stoll recalls, their standard bourbon, nothing special.

It was made in the big distillery, not the barrel-a-day-distillery, which had yet to be built.

In contract distilling, a spirit is made to a customer's specifications for a certain pre-agreed price. Terms can vary but when the customer pays the contracted amount, the product becomes the customer's property, even though it is still in the maker's possession.

Some customers take immediate delivery of new make and either use it as green (i.e., un-aged) whiskey in a blend or age it themselves. If they are going to age it they may have it delivered in a tanker and barrel it themselves. Most contract distilling customers do neither. Instead, they pay the distillery to barrel and store the whiskey while it ages. They also pay the taxes. They only take delivery when the whisky reaches its desired maturity and is ready to sell. They may even have the distillery bottle it for them and take it as case goods.

The odd thing about the Hirsch contract is that for 15 years, Hirsch paid the annual fees and taxes but never asked for the whiskey to be withdrawn. As part of their maturation service, distilleries typically monitor (i.e., periodically taste) the whiskey in their care so they can determine how it's aging and inform the owner of its condition. Hirsch probably was informed, therefore, that the whiskey was in excellent shape and could remain in wood.

Even so, 15 years is very old for a bourbon, especially then.

When Michter's began its final decline, the bank specifically instructed Dick Stoll to make sure Hirsch got his whiskey out of there. They did not want to be responsible for any damage to Hirsch's property. This suggests that Hirsch's whiskey was the only contracted whiskey still in the Michter's warehouses by then. Only when pressed did Hirsch begin to look for a buyer.

That's where Gordon Hue comes in. Hue was a retailer, but on the side he bottled and exported long-aged bourbon to Japan, where it suddenly had become popular. That's what he intended to do with Hirsch's 400 barrels of 15-year-old bourbon. It was a sweet business. The Japanese were suddenly crazy for very old bourbon and willing to pay top dollar for it, but most people who had old bourbon were willing to sell it cheap, because the U.S.-market wasn't interested. As the middleman, Hue could pocket the difference without doing very much work, or so it must have seemed.

Stoll supervised the loading and shipment of Hirsch's 400 barrels to a winery in Cincinnati on Hue's behalf. Stoll remembers this as 1990 but there is strong evidence that at least some of it was shipped in 1989, possibly even 1988. It's very possible that Hue did not buy it all at once, or at least didn't take delivery all at once. It is also likely that some of the first shipments went directly to Julian Van Winkle's place in Lawrenceburg, Kentucky, for immediate bottling, not to Cincinnati.

It was definitely all gone before the bank pulled the plug on Valentine's Day, 1990.

A few years later, the bank hired Stoll to do an inventory of the whiskey (and some raisin brandy) that was still in the warehouses at Michter's. He counted about 40,000 barrels, which (in relation to the newspaper stories quoted earlier) is a bit less than 2 *million* gallons, not 300,000.

How could the newspaper reports get it so wrong? It is likely that the newspaper's source was a Lebanon County official, who was probably estimating (i.e., guessing) based on what he or she had seen or had reported to them by, perhaps, county law enforcement. There clearly was not an inventory at that point, else why was Stoll later hired to conduct one?

That number sounds about right. If we assume the distillery was filling 50 barrels a day toward the end, and running for about 120 days a year (we know they were running at about one-third capacity), that's 6,000 barrels a year. Times four years, that's 24,000 barrels. Times six is 36,000.

Sometime after the inventory, Stoll was again hired by the bank to supervise the loading of the remaining barrels, which emptied the warehouses. He recalls calling the electric company to get power turned on for the elevators. He doesn't know where that whiskey went. He heard a rumor that it was redistilled into racing fuel.

That, too, sounds about right. When whiskey can't be sold as whiskey for any reason, it typically is redistilled into grain neutral spirit (GNS), either for beverage or industrial uses, including fuel. Redistillation strips it of any unique character it might have had and reduces it to mere alcohol, i.e., ethanol. GNS brings a much lower price than whiskey, even bad whiskey.

On the beverage side, GNS is used for vodka, gin, and liqueurs. On the industrial side, it is used for medicines, solvents, preservatives, and fuel.

It's probable that the county got so desperate that it offered the whiskey free to anyone who had the proper license and would take it and haul it away, and a re-distiller did. Ethanol fuel is used in IndyCar Series racing, so 'racing fuel' is plausible, or it may have been someone's euphemism for grain neutral spirits.

With the warehouses empty, it was just real estate. The county sold the property for taxes, at a negotiated and likely very discounted rate. The new owner auctioned off everything of value, including the barrel-a-day distillery sold to David Beam. The land was sold again in 1999. That owner struggled to find a use for the property and was finally ordered by the county, which considered it a safety hazard, to either clean it up or sell it. In 2011, he sold it to JJC Investments, which owns an adjacent property. They said they intended to repair the buildings enough to rent them out as storage space, but have demolished most of them instead. No one is talking about restoring anything or returning to distilling.

The bronze plaques that proclaimed Michter's to be a National Historic Landmark were stolen years ago. Nothing marks the property today, not even a roadside historic marker. Nothing.

But one small part of Michter's lives on and is once again making whiskey.

In February of 2011, David Beam sold most of the barrel-a-day distillery equipment, including the two copper pot stills, to Tom's Foolery Distillery outside of Cleveland, Ohio. That fall Dick Stoll, the only man to operate the barrel-a-day distillery, was reunited with it at Tom and Lianne Herbruck's behest. Both Stoll and David Beam, along with Beam's sons and grandsons, are helping the Herbrucks get the barrel-a-day distillery going again.

The Herbruck family's Tom's Foolery Distillery began with two smaller stills, with which they made apple brandy. They aged it in oak, including used bourbon barrels. Their small annual output of Tom's Foolery Applejack sells out quickly in the Cleveland area. In late 2011, they switched the apple brandy production to the Michter's stills and later that winter began to make bourbon whiskey in them too.

In April, 2012, David Beam's teenage grandson, Ben, served a one-week internship at Tom's Foolery, learning how to run the Michter's barrel-a-day equipment. At the end of the week, David Beam, Ben's father Bill, and other family members traveled from Kentucky to Cleveland to pick up Ben and see (and taste) the fruits of his training. Just as Everett Beam once traveled to Pennsylvania to continue his distilling career, a new generation of Beams is continuing their ancestral craft in rural Cuyahoga County.

The Michter's barrel-a-day distillery consists of a 500 gallon beer still and a 110 gallon spirit still, a condenser, associated tanks, try boxes, and other parts. There are three 500 gallon cypress fermenters, two of which have been refurbished and are in service. The cooker is only 250 gallons, so it takes two cooks to fill each fermenter. About 60 gallons of the cooking liquid in each batch is backset, spent mash from the previous distillation. All this makes Tom's Foolery one of the few micro-distilleries making traditional double-distilled sour mash bourbon.

But back to the Hirsch bourbon, made in 1974. One big question remains. *Why* was it made in the first place? The most plausible theory, considering his long history with the distillery, and with Forman and Glass personally, is that Hirsch contracted for the whiskey, not because he had any use for it (as evidenced by his later behavior with regard to it), but as a way to infuse some emergency capital into Pennco, which failed soon thereafter despite his help.

Rather than investing in the struggling distillery directly, and losing everything if it failed, this gave him something that would hold at least some of its value, regardless of the distillery's ultimate fortunes. In this he was not unlike the farmer-distillers of Johann

Shenk's day, making whiskey to preserve the value of their grain.

By the end, Forman and Glass were long gone so, when pressed, Hirsch sought and found a buyer for his then 15-year-old bourbon whiskey. It so happened that it had turned out rather nicely.

13. The Pot Still Claim.

There is an old joke involving a New Orleans street vendor. "Hot pies, get your hot pies here," he shouts.

A man approaches. "I'll take one of those pies," says the man.

They transact their business and the man immediately bites into the pie. Just as fast, he spits it out. "Why, this pie is *ice cold,*" he complains.

"Yes, sir. I know," replies the vendor. "When I say 'Hot Pie,' I don't mean the *pie* is hot. 'Hot Pie' is just the *name* of that pie."

From the time he created the Michter's brand, Louis Forman had put the words 'old-fashioned pot still' on his jugs and, later, bottles. But was Michter's whiskey, and by extension A. H. Hirsch Reserve Bourbon, ever really made in pot stills 'the old-fashioned way'?

The answer is yes *and* no, but mostly no.

It's possible this fact will disappoint many of the whiskey's most ardent fans. They thought it explained the whiskey's excellence. But the whiskey is no less excellent because it wasn't really made in pot stills the old-fashioned way. It stands on its own merits.

What's so great about pot stills? Although it is a miniscule part of the whiskey marketplace, single malt scotch is the straw that stirs the drink. Single malt scotch is what people want to talk about, learn about, sample and collect. Single malt scotch is expensive and very profitable for the producers, distributors, and retailers of it. Single malt scotch is made in pot stills.

Being made in pot stills does not necessarily make single malt scotch superior to other types of whiskey, but don't try to tell that to a single malt scotch enthusiast. Today's emerging micro-distillers also swear by pot stills, even though few use them. A true pot still, of the type used in Scotland, is known as an alembic still. An alembic is a very simple still, a pot with a tight-fitting lid, with a spout of some kind at the top of the lid to steer the vapors into the condenser.

What most micro-distillers call a pot still is actually a hybrid; a batch still like an alembic, that has rectification plates like a column still.

Alembics, the true 'old fashioned' style of pot still, are used to make single malt scotch whiskey and also Cognac brandy, so they have a pretty good track record.

Unfortunately, the Michter's pot still claim is one that even the distillery's own brochures from as early as 1964 effectively refute. When they describe Michter's whiskey-making process, they say that after fermentation the distillers beer "is sent through the column still." This produces 'high wine,' which is then "distilled in the pot still."

This describes exactly the conventional double-distillation system practiced by virtually all American whiskey distilleries, then and now. This is how bourbon whiskey has been made for more than 100 years. The fermented mash, known as distiller's beer, is distilled first in a column still. This captures all of the alcohol and, when the vapor is condensed, produces a solution with the desired alcohol content, typically between 60 and 70 percent alcohol by volume (ABV).

This solution is then introduced into a pot still in a second step that distillers say 'polishes' the spirit, by removing the most stubborn unpleasant congeners. This step has little effect on alcohol content, it is strictly done to make the spirit taste better. American distillers call this second still either a 'doubler' or a 'thumper,' but it *is* a pot still. It's even an *alembic* still.

In a 1980 Michter's brochure, there is a photograph of what appears to be a conventional American whiskey doubler, of the sort you can find in any American whiskey distillery today. Painted on the side of the tank is 'Pot Still Doubler No. 1.'

Describing the doubler as a pot still is a legitimate way for any American distiller to work the term 'pot still' into its production explanation. Since the doubler gives the new make spirit its final, pre-aging taste profile, it is arguably the more important of the two distillations.

From Dick Stoll and other sources, we know that Kirk's-Pennco-Michter's – the distillery as it was set up by Everett Beam – did one thing that was unique. The typical doubler in Kentucky and Tennessee works in-line with the column still as a single system. At Michter's, the doubler was separate and operated separately. The column still's output went into a holding tank for later introduction into the pot still doubler. Doubling separately allowed the distiller to make heads and tails cuts. Unlike most distillers they discarded the heads and tails rather than redistilling them.

Does any of the above justify the Michter's 'old-fashioned pot still' claim?

Not really.

Expect for running the doubler independent of the column still, Kirk's-Pennco-Michter's didn't do anything that distinguished it from other distilleries. The distillery that came back after Prohibition, possibly as early as 1937, that operated until February, 1990, was for the most part a conventional American whiskey distillery.

There was a period after World War II when some producers did not perform the second distillation, hence they did not use a pot still to make their whiskey. This was done to save money. Although widespread, single distillation of bourbon and other whiskeys was never universal. There was never a time when Kirk's-Pennco-Michter's was the *only* distillery in America that double-distilled, although it may have been the only one in Pennsylvania during the industry's rush to cheapness that began in the late 1960s.

Even then, most whiskey distilleries kept using doublers. Eventually, what was left of the industry realized that doublers are essential for quality whiskey and double-distillation has been standard practice ever since. This is true of the major distilleries only. Most micro-distilleries don't double.

We know very little about the distillery set-up at Schaefferstown *before* Everett Beam got there. The double-distillation system described above only became common in the United States after the 1860s, so it would have been all-pot before then. Was it ever all-pot *after* Prohibition? Most likely not until 1976 when the barrel-a-day distillery was installed.

Louis Forman and Everett Beam probably *intended* in 1950-51 to make a true pot-distilled whiskey, i.e., an all-pot whiskey like that made at Woodford Reserve Distillery in Versailles, Kentucky. There, whiskey is made entirely in pot stills, three in series.

They *intended* to do it, they may even have *tried* to do it, but for some reason they didn't succeed. Instead they just *said* it. There is no evidence that 'pot distilled' was ever anything more than a slogan, loosely supported by their use of the pot still doubler, and by the unique *way* they used it, which modern distillers say would have made a difference in how the whiskey tasted. Nevertheless, no one who worked at or visited Michter's has ever reported seeing any evidence of an all-pot operation there before 1976.

'Old fashioned pot still' wasn't a lie, but it sure wasn't the truth.

It is similar to the 'sour mash' claim. Every major whiskey distillery in America uses the sour mash process, but only a few emblazon the words 'sour mash' on their label. Mitcher's did, probably in emulation of Jack Daniel's, which still does. Many consumers believe Jack Daniels is special because it is 'sour mash' whiskey. It isn't. Jim Beam is sour mash whiskey, so are Evan Williams, Maker's Mark, Wild Turkey, and just about any other bourbon or rye you can name. It is as if a car manufacturer promoted the fact that *its* vehicles all use *internal* combustion engines.

Preiss Imports, the last company to market A. H. Hirsch Bourbon, called it "the oldest available pot distilled bourbon in America." They further said it "hail(ed) from the time-honored pot-still tradition; slow, costly, work intensive, but a delicious relic of American history." They claimed that Michter's made, "the only post-Prohibition pot still Bourbon in America."

None of that was true. Preiss simply took the words "old-fashioned pot still" and ran with them, describing what would have been the case if it had been an all-alembic pot still operation, which it wasn't.

If using a doubler makes whiskey pot-distilled, then every major brand of American bourbon and rye made today is pot-distilled. Although the A. H. Hirsch Reserve Bourbon wasn't the same recipe as Michter's Original Sour Mash Whiskey, it was made the same way. Neither whiskey was distilled in an all-pot-still system.

In fairness to the folks at Preiss Imports, who were very generous and helpful in the research for this story, and never tried to hide anything, they just repeated what they were told.

Although the pot still claim was never true, it ultimately didn't matter because the Hirsch bourbon was truly exceptional. That is ultimately what made it a legend, not the bogus pot still claim. We'll get into that in more detail before we're through.

14. The A. H. Hirsch Brand Is Born.

A crucial source for this chapter was Julian P. Van Winkle, III. He is the grandson of 'Pappy' Van Winkle, who established the Stitzel-Weller Distillery in Louisville right after Prohibition.

When the Van Winkle family sold Stitzel-Weller in 1972, Julian's father started a new company. He bought whiskey in bulk from the old family distillery and bottled it as Old Rip Van Winkle Bourbon. Old Rip was a minor Stitzel-Weller brand that the family had retained in the sale. The name also had sentimental meaning, as 'Rip' was his sister's nickname. J. P. Van Winkle Jr. also did private label bottling. Another asset he kept was the Stitzel-Weller Company's customer list.

The new owners didn't seem to mind. Van Winkle mostly did small jobs they didn't care about. They even allowed him to operate his business out of the Stitzel-Weller Distillery.

After his father's death in 1981, Julian P. Van Winkle III took over the business but was forced to relocate. He purchased the old Hoffman Distillery near Lawrenceburg, not to distill but to age and bottle whiskey for himself and others, continuing his father's business but also adding to it. The business was very small. His only full-time employee was a bookkeeper.

With his own bottling line, Van Winkle could do contract bottling of whiskey other than Stitzel-Weller's and get more business that way. To bottle distilled spirits you need bottling line equipment, of course, but you also need a distilled spirits producer (DSP) permit from the Federal government. That makes distilled spirits bottling a specialty. The local Pepsi bottler can't bottle distilled spirits.

So it was that in 1989, Gordon Hue contracted with Julian P. Van Winkle III for Van Winkle to bottle Hue's new brand, A. H. Hirsch Reserve. Between 1989 and 1995, in dribs and drabs, Van Winkle bottled 1,744 cases of the Pennsylvania bourbon for Gordon Hue, the brand's owner. It was just a contract bottling job, Van Winkle never had a piece of the business, but he did taste the whiskey and offer Hue advice.

It is on that relatively small amount of whiskey that the legend of A. H. Hirsch Reserve was based.

When Preiss Imports bought the A. H. Hirsch brand and remaining whiskey from the Hue family, they received some interesting documents. One is a warehouse receipt dated June 6, 1988, for 19 barrels of bourbon distilled at Pennco Distillers, Inc. of Pennsylvania on February 27, 1974. A warehouse receipt can be merely proof of ownership, but it can also be used to transfer whiskey to a new owner, like an automobile title. This receipt may represent the first batch of whiskey purchased from Hirsch by Gordon Hue.

The other document is a handwritten 'biographical sketch' of Adolph Hirsch, dated September 12, 1989, and written by Hirsch's wife. Presumably, it is something Hue requested and Mrs. Hirsch provided. It is the basis for the previous biographical chapter about Hirsch.

Mr. and Mrs. Hirsch were then living in Grand Rapids, Michigan. Adolph Hirsch would have been 81 at the time. At the bottom of the biographical sketch is written the year 1974, below which is the following statement: "Mr. Hirsch is extremely proud of the high quality and character of this stock of bourbon, and would be pleased to have his name associated with the product."

Thus A. H. Hirsch Reserve was officially born, in September of 1989.

Pennco, the company that made the bourbon for Hirsch in 1974, had thrived through the mid-1960s, but by the end of that decade it was beginning to struggle, as were most American whiskey distilleries at the time. By 1969, Pennco was operating at about half of its capacity and begging the county for tax relief, as reported in the local newspaper. Inflation was pushing up interest rates, which hit whiskey distilleries especially hard because of their constant need to finance aging stock.

Worst of all, American whiskey sales were tanking across the land, as consumers increasingly turned to lighter imported whiskeys, as well as neutral or nearly-neutral spirits such as gin, vodka, and rum, which are easier to use in mixed drinks. Many younger consumers had begun to experiment with tequila and with illegal, non-liquid intoxicants. Whiskey-makers all across the country were going out of business, either through acquisition or closure. For 18 months spanning

1970 and 1971, Pennco stopped distilling altogether, although the plant continued to bottle and sell whiskey from its inventory.

When distilling resumed in late 1971 the new venture wasn't whiskey, it was raisin brandy, an additive used by vintners for fortified wines such as sherry and port. It was the first of many schemes conceived to keep the Schaefferstown distillery afloat.

Historically, distilleries do not operate during the hottest months of summer, and they usually take a long break at the end of the year. Consequently, they traditionally divide the year into two six-month distilling seasons, spring and fall. Because output is controlled primarily through days of operation, distillers base the actual start and end date of each season on their production needs.

All of the bourbon whiskey that became A. H. Hirsch Reserve was distilled during the spring 1974, distilling season, meaning it was made between January 1 and June 30 of that year. In fact, we know from the surviving warehouse receipt that it was made at the end of February, perhaps extending into the first week of March. You have to be careful talking to distillers because they will refer to something as being made "in the spring," even when, like the Hirsch, it was actually made in February, because it was made during the six-month spring distilling season.

Here is what else we know about the circumstances of the whiskey's manufacture. We know its production was overseen by Dick Stoll using Everett Beam's bourbon mash bill of 75 percent corn, 13 percent rye, and 12 percent malt. No big surprise, that's a pretty standard mash bill, especially for that period. Today, most of the top brands use a little less of the more costly rye and malt, so they're closer to 80 percent corn.

Stoll says the bourbon they made for Hirsch wasn't unusual. It was the same bourbon they made for everybody.

Hirsch's order came to about 23-thousand proof gallons. A 'proof gallon' is one gallon of 100° proof (50% ABV) spirit. Proof gallon is the unit of measurement upon which taxes are based. The original distillation proof, according to the 1988 warehouse receipt, was 115° proof, low by modern standards.

Hirsch paid to have the bourbon made and paid storage charges on it for the next 15 years, as well as taxes. We don't know how much he paid, but just to put the numbers in perspective, assume a cost of $5 per proof gallon. That's $115,000.

The warehouse receipt tells us that, in 1988, Michter's was charging 25¢ per barrel per month for storage. That comes to $1,200 a year for 400 barrels. We can assume that Pennsylvania levied some kind of annual state tax on the whiskey in storage. (Kentucky does.) Regardless of how much it cost, we know Hirsch was content to pay the freight and leave his bourbon in the Michter's warehouses until that became impossible.

Why did he keep it so long and why it was made in the first place?

We don't know the answer to either question. The most credible theory is that Hirsch contracted for it primarily as a way to infuse some cash into the struggling company, a company with which he had

had a relationship for more than 30 years. He could have sold the whiskey when it matured, after four or five years, not perhaps for as much as he would have liked in a down market, but he could have gotten out from under the annual taxes and fees. Instead he sent Michter's an annual check for the next 15 years.

Hirsch was 66-years-old in 1974 and by all indications a very wealthy man. The sum he invested in his 400 barrels of bourbon probably didn't matter to him. It may, in his mind, have been done primarily as a favor to an old friend. He also, like many, may have felt the industry was on the verge of recovery and that when his bourbon matured, there would be a market for it.

Even if it was a favor, Hirsch was still a businessman. He wasn't particularly concerned about making money but he didn't want to throw it away either. By buying whiskey instead of stock in the company he assured himself some sort of return, however uncertain the amount. It's hard to imagine he intended to sit on it for 15 years. It was probably just easier for him to write a check each year than to deal with it.

Fifteen years later, when the end came for Michter's and Hirsch finally had to find a customer for his whiskey, lest he lose it in the chaos that was sure to follow, he found Gordon Hue, who with his father and brothers ran a large liquor store in Covington, Kentucky, called the Cork and Bottle.

As a sideline to his retail operation, Gordon Hue had been bottling extra-aged whiskey and selling it for high prices in Japan and other international markets since about 1984. What the Japanese wanted was

American whiskey aged for durations similar to those of scotch whisky, the older the better, but at least 12- to maybe 15-years-old. Since American whiskey at that time was typically sold at 4- to 8-years-old, 12-year-old bourbon shouldn't exist. But because of the industry's decline there was, in fact, an excess of whiskey made in the 1970s that was getting awfully long in the tooth by the mid-1980s.

The sudden Japanese interest in extra-aged bourbon, and in bourbon in general, was the first good news bourbon makers had heard in 15 years.

Hue bought Hirsch's 400 barrels and got it out of Pennsylvania before the final ownership group abandoned the place. We don't know how much he paid for it but he undoubtedly got a good deal.

Although Hue wasn't the first bottler-exporter to enter the Japanese market with extra-aged bourbon, he was early. There is, however, no evidence that anyone bid against him for the Hirsch bourbon.

The first barrels from Schaefferstown arrived at Julian Van Winkle's facility in Lawrenceburg, Kentucky, in September of 1989.

These dates and other numbers are very reliable because they come directly from Van Winkle's ledger books.

That first batch of 47 cases was a 15-year-old bourbon bottled at 95.6° proof. Some of it was sold at the Hue's Covington store, the rest went overseas. In December, another 134 cases were bottled at the same age and proof, followed by 340 cases in February of 1990.

Although the whiskey had all turned 16-years-old by March of 1990, it continued to be bottled as a 15-

year-old until April of 1991, probably to avoid printing new labels. In April, 1991, the first 16-year-old was bottled. To distinguish this 16-year-old from the later bottling, just look for 'Lawrenceburg, Kentucky' on the label. The later, 2003 bottling says 'Frankfort, Kentucky.'

Every few months, Hue would send Van Winkle another bottling order, 57 cases in April of 1991, 200 more that November. Hue also had Van Winkle bottle 100 cases of it as a brand called Colonel Randolph, and some more under the name Old Gromes.

Before Michter's closed in February of 1990, the rest of the 400 barrels were shipped to a winery in Cincinnati. Not long after all of the bourbon had passed its 16th birthday, Van Winkle and Hue decided that most of it was as good as it was going to get. To stop it from aging any further, about 3,000 proof gallons were dumped into a stainless steel tank at the winery. Van Winkle still had some of the first batch in Lawrenceburg, in barrels, though only a few of them. That bourbon was allowed to remain in wood in Van Winkle's warehouse, some of it until it turned 20 years old.

In November of 1992, some of those barrels were dumped to produce 37 cases of 18-year-old, 93° proof Hirsch. That December, Van Winkle bottled up the last of the 16-year-old that he had tanked in 1990, about eight cases as A. H. Hirsch, some more as Boones Knoll, for the first time at 91.6° proof.

After that, the 16-year-old bourbon arrived at Lawrenceburg in tank trucks from Cincinnati, enough in July of 1993 for 300 cases (at 95.6° proof).

That November it was back to the remaining barrels, for 121 cases of 19-year-old at 93° proof. The last barrels were dumped and bottled between December of 1994 and April of 1995, producing 500 cases of a 20-year-old at 91.6° proof.

It is clear from these numbers that although the whiskey was selling steadily, it was not blowing the doors off. Japanese consumers liked that sort of thing, but the product was extremely expensive there. It was more affordable in the U.S. but still high for an American whiskey. At that time the bourbon renaissance was barely in its infancy and Hue did very little to promote the brand. The fact that this tiny brand was marketing five different expressions probably didn't help.

It seems doubtful that when Hue bought the whiskey in 1988 and 1989, he anticipated that most of it would still be in his possession six years later.

It may be that Gordon Hue never had the capacity to distribute and promote his products thoroughly in Japan, let alone in the much larger, and less hospitable, U.S. market. He had an excellent product but may have been in over his head, business-wise.

That 1995 bottling of the 20 year old was the last of the A. H. Hirsch bourbon bottled by Van Winkle at Lawrenceburg. It was also the end of the line for Gordon Hue. The other Hues ran the brand for a little while longer, then sold it to Henry Preiss. By this time it had gained an international reputation among American whiskey enthusiasts as an exceptionally fine bourbon whiskey.

If any of the Hirsch bourbon was bottled and sold between 1995 and 2003, we have no record of it. It's possible the Hues had sufficient case goods to last through that period. We only know how many cases Van Winkle bottled and, subsequently, how much Buffalo Trace bottled. We don't know how many cases the Hues sold, nor when, nor how many they had left when Preiss entered the picture.

The whiskey we know about seems pretty well accounted for by the bottlings we know about. If anything else was bottled during those eight years, it couldn't have been very much.

In 2002, Van Winkle closed his operation in Lawrenceburg and moved his business to Buffalo Trace, in Frankfort.

The remaining Hirsch bourbon, the stash that had been tanked in Cincinnati, also went to Buffalo Trace. In 2003, after 12 years in stainless steel, Preiss had the last of it bottled. It came to 2,500 cases, more than all of the previous production combined. That is the 16-year-old, 91.6° proof, gold capsule product that many people own and that still shows up occasionally at retail. It is the package we described in detail in Chapter 11. It *is* A. H. Hirsch Reserve to most people.

In the next three years, Preiss sold 1,500 cases. In the following three years, he sold most of the remaining 1,000 cases. In 2009, Preiss un-bottled what was left and transferred it into crystal decanters for a special $1,500 farewell package. We don't know how many cases of that there were, but we know it was probably no more than a couple hundred. That was it. All of that 1974 bourbon, all 400 barrels, finally had been sold to at least the distributor level. As far as Preiss was concerned, the story was over.

Or was it? While Preiss decided not to sully the *A. H.* Hirsch name, he proceeded to give the Hirsch name, without the initials, a hard workout. There were ryes, Canadians, and more; mostly extra-aged, mostly one-offs produced from found batches of orphaned whiskey. They were all labeled properly, but no doubt there were a few people who bought them thinking they were that Hirsch bourbon they had heard so much about.

Adolph Hirsch's 400 barrels of bourbon, minus 15-20 years of evaporation, translated into about 4,244 cases of A. H. Hirsch Reserve Straight Bourbon Whiskey, at assorted ages and proofs, and an unknown number of bottles that were released as other brands. The whiskey we can account for amounts to about 44 percent of what was made. Assuming that about half of the original volume was lost due to evaporation, that's pretty close. It's a tiny amount of whiskey for such a big reputation, especially when you consider that it took almost 20 years to sell it all through the distribution system.

So it was a unique product, with many twists and turns involved along its road to market. But was it really that good?

16. Synchronicity.

In the 1920s, the Swiss psychiatrist Carl Gustav Jung coined the word 'synchronicity' to describe what he called "temporally coincident occurrences of acausal events." Most people know it as a song and album by the Police, released in 1982.

Coincidentally or not, 1982 is also the year Lew Bryson discovered the Michter's Distillery.

The bourbon that would become A. H. Hirsch Reserve was then 8 years old, but he didn't know that.

Today, Bryson is managing editor of *The Whisky Advocate*, America's leading whisky publication, the premier source for whisky information, education and entertainment for whisky enthusiasts. *Whisky Advocate* also sponsors WhiskyFest, the country's largest and most respected whisky tasting events.

But Bryson, coincidentally, grew up near Michter's, just a few miles south of the distillery, although he was oblivious to that fact until an unseasonably warm day in late December, 1982, when he took an impromptu road trip with a buddy. There is a good chance the song "Synchronicity" was playing on the radio.

John Hansell, Bryson's boss, who founded the magazine more than 20 years ago, not long after Michter's died, and is still its editor and publisher today, grew up even closer to Michter's, in Lebanon. He, too, was unaware of the local whiskey-maker until many years later. He must not have had Mrs. Stoll as a teacher in school. Today Hansell lives and publishes *The Whiskey Advocate* about an hour from Schaefferstown in tiny Emmaus, Pennsylvania.

I am a contributor to *Whisky Advocate* and have known both Hansell and Bryson for years.

"I almost literally stumbled across the distillery outside of Schaefferstown one day in 1982 while joy-riding with my friend Bobby Gryce," wrote Bryson recently, at my request. "I grew up not far from there, but had never heard of Michter's; certainly didn't know there was a whiskey distillery folded away in the hills up there.

"Bobby and I took off one afternoon in late December when the weather was unseasonably warm and sunny, to blow off the stink of being cooped up for a couple cold months. I wasn't a whiskey drinker at the time, but I was a drinker, so when we saw the signs for a distillery tour, the wheel easily turned in my hands to head that way. We weren't the only ones out that fine, fine day; the place was hopping, and we got a tour with about ten other people.

"I wish I could remember more of that visit, other than the beautiful sunlight and the tiny place nestled by the small creek, but I was 23 at the time and mostly interested in beer. I do remember thinking $10 for a bottle of bourbon was a lot...sigh.

"It was fun, but we had more fun after we drove on, hitting countryside bars, and seeing the equally old Yuengling brewery for the first time that same day; it was a *good* day. I didn't think much more about the

place for years, other than to note that it had closed –
saw a newspaper article – and to tell myself that if it
was close by, of course, it couldn't possibly be any
good.

"That all changed when I had my first taste of the
A.H. Hirsch 16 year old bottling of Michter's in the
1990s. I had learned to love bourbon by then, and this
stuff was an eye-opener. Since then I've been back to
see the old moldering buildings, and felt feelings of
sadness and anger at their state. I've bought more
bottles of the 16 year old than any other non-standard
whiskey in my life. I still share some of my dwindling
stock whenever anyone who appreciates whiskey
visits my house. And I still feel a real sense of pride
that Pennsylvania whiskey tastes that good...no matter
how it was made."

John Hansell discovered Michter's whiskey about
18 months before Bryson discovered the distillery. He
bought a bottle shortly after his 21st birthday in 1981,
while working a summer job in King of Prussia, which
is just outside of Philadelphia. He was an
undergraduate at Penn State then and no longer living
in Lebanon County.

"I enjoyed it. I wasn't blown away by it," wrote
Hansell in response to my questions. "I appreciated it
more because of the fact that it was made in
Pennsylvania, and in the county where I grew up."

That was Michter's Original Sour Mash, a different
whiskey. Hansell discovered A. H. Hirsch Reserve in
1992. He bought a bottle of the 18-year-old at Park
Avenue Liquors in New York City. Later he bought the
more common 16- and 20-year-old bottlings. "My
favorite is the 16," he says. "Still, I have always had an

emotional attachment to any whiskey from the Michter's distillery. My favorite bottle is actually a ½ gallon Bicentenary Jug, which I assume was bottled around 1976. I actually found it in a hole in the wall liquor store outside of Boston in a box on a high shelf next to a bunch of Beam decanters. I still haven't opened it, but plan on doing so very soon."

Sam Komlenic is another *Whisky Advocate* employee with deep Pennsylvania roots and a fascination with the state's distilling history, including Michter's. He is the magazine's copy editor. Komlenic grew up in Westmoreland County, home to the Gibson and Dillinger Distilleries. He now lives in State College and was on his way there, following a trip to Philadelphia, when he discovered Michter's in 1979.

"Michter's was (and still is) located in a very rural part of Lebanon County," wrote Komlenic. "No developments around, no major highways, no railroad connections; just a big distillery in the middle of a lot of cows and farmland. In the 70s, it was quite the tourist attraction, even offering donkey rides for the kids. The tour started in the visitor center, which was also the souvenir shop adjacent to the Jug House, where they sold the whiskey.

"The tour cost a dollar and included the distillery, Bomberger's original bonded warehouse (that had been converted to interpretive display space), and the old Bomberger distillery, which held the small pot still setup that was built for the American bicentennial. At the end of the tour, your guide took a picture of you with the whiskey you had (hopefully) bought, and sent you the photo with a thank-you note. I still have mine. Back then, Michter's was the only distillery in the country selling whiskey on-site, by special historical exemption written into the Pennsylvania Liquor Code."

Komlenic visited several more times, including once in 1989, shortly before it closed, and again in 1990, after it did. During his 1989 visit he met Dick Stoll, with whom he was reunited during another visit in 2010.

Ethan Smith is a younger man, with no connection to *Whisky Advocate,* who also grew up near Michter's, still lives there, and has become one of its most ardent champions. He organized the gathering that reunited Sam Komlenic and Dick Stoll, and also introduced me to Stoll. He collected and archived many of the documents referenced in this book.

As a child, Smith discovered Michter's on a tourism poster in a gas station, but his anti-alcohol mother wouldn't hear of visiting. He also remembers seeing a TV news story about it when it closed. It mentioned the looting and vandalism problems they were having.

Now we have to fast-forward 20 years for Smith's next Michter's memory.

"While picking around online about local history, I ran across a few websites where people did exploration of abandoned buildings and it sparked my interest. I started to think of abandoned places around here and one of the first was Michter's. So the research began: Who owns it? What was it like back when it was operating? What products did they make? What is the future of the site? As my research unfolded, I found myself hunting down the decanters. Then came the paperwork. Then ex-employees. Then trying to preserve the site. It just snowballed from there.

My first impressions of Michter's were of absolute amazement. How could someone let all this history go to waste? Why wasn't the local historical society trying to preserve what's left? How could a National Historic Landmark and National Historic Place be left to rot and collapse? After touring the distillery with Dwight Hostetter (who owned it at the time), I was in love with the place. The same attention to process and detail was given to each and every product that left the small distillery. Dick Stoll told me this over dinner. He's proud of what he and Everett Beam distilled, whether it was $9 per bottle Michter's or $500 per bottle A.H. Hirsch.

"Dwight finally sold the distillery to a local refuse and recycling company and they have started demolition of most of the distillery. They claimed in a Lebanon Daily News article that they would be keeping a few of the buildings for use as storage space. It's hard for me to drive back Michter's Road now and see empty concrete pads and dirt mounds where there were once buildings. It hurts. My wife and I tried the best we could with our limited resources to stave off the seemingly inevitable end of the distillery. But in the end, we were no match for 'progress.'"

Is all this passion for Michter's an example of synchronicity? The common thread in the experiences of these four men and others like them is love of whiskey and Pennsylvania roots, leading to the discovery of a renowned Pennsylvania whiskey maker that hung on longer than most – longer than anyone at 237 years – but died a generation ago and is now largely forgotten.

Businesses operate in a public sphere and often have effects on people that are unknown and unintended. As today's booming macro- and micro-distilleries demonstrate, there is something emotionally compelling about alcohol-makers. People by the thousands don't flock to Lynchburg, Tennessee, or Loretto, Kentucky, just to see how whiskey is made. It is more on the order of a pilgrimage, a desire humans feel to have physical communion with places where something happens, or has happened, that is important to them. Most people don't take trips to see where their food is grown or where their furniture was made, but many want to see where their favorite beer, wine, or whiskey is made.

There may be nothing left to see at Michter's but there is plenty left to feel.

16. Epilogue And Tasting.

A. H. Hirsch Special Reserve Straight Bourbon Whiskey will always be compared to the primary product of the distillery that made it, Michter's Original Sour Mash Whiskey. They were very different products. Michter's was *not* bourbon and contained three times as much rye as the Hirsch bourbon. The Hirsch was aged entirely in new charred oak barrels while some of the Michter's was aged in used barrels. The Michter's was aged for four to six years. The Hirsch was aged for 15 to 20. A bottle of Michter's Original Sour Mash cost about the same as a bottle of Jack Daniel's or Jim Beam. A. H. Hirsch Reserve was always one of the most expensive bourbons you could buy.

Michter's wasn't bad whiskey. Everett Beam and Dick Stoll were very proud of both products. Michael Jackson called Michter's Original Sour Mash, "a delicious and distinctive whiskey with a full, smooth palate, sweet but clean, and a flavorful, almost gingery, crisp, dry finish." He also reported that it had almost no distribution by 1986-87, its sales coming primarily from the distillery gift shop.

Primarily, perhaps, but not exclusively. I found several of the round glass bottles, at 86 proof (43% ABV), in a liquor store on the southwest side of Chicago in the mid-1990s. There was no mistaking it for the Hirsch, which I had also discovered by then, but it had its own charm. It reminded me of Jim Beam Rye.

For any distillery, large or small, making whiskey and putting it into wood is an act of faith, especially when your mature whiskey isn't selling very well. Distilleries may cut back on production but they can't quit altogether. When you stop feeding the aging pipeline, that's surrender. It's only a matter of time until you're out of business. So distillery inventories build up during bad years. Everyone has faith the recovery is right around the corner so they keep making whiskey. They have to. Only when they have a several year oversupply, or run out of money, do they stop.

When American whiskey began its dramatic sales slump in the late 1960s, a slump that continued for 20 years, a 'bubble' of excess inventory was created in the industry pipeline. It was a glut that would last for decades. Most distillers then and still believe American whiskey becomes over-aged after about eight years in wood, but suddenly there was a vast amount of whiskey aged ten years and more sitting in the warehouses. To everyone's surprise it found a market, first overseas and then here, and a lucrative market at that, at least as represented by retail prices.

Most remarkably, consumers decided they liked 'over-aged' whiskey. It wasn't just a novelty. In time, they would find they liked other products the industry never thought would fly, like straight releases of flavoring whiskeys created for blends, but that's a different story.

These very expensive, very old bourbons and ryes always represented a very small market; profitable, but small in volume terms. They were like the Islay Malts of bourbon, even rarer because so many were one-offs. Heaven Hill's Elijah Craig 18-year-old was a rare example of a teenage bourbon with a fully stoked pipeline, yet it too has hit the wall. The brand was discontinued in 2012 and will only reappear from time to time as a limited edition.

Hirsch is a perfect representative of the glut era extra-aged one-offs. Always well-regarded, and written about thousands of times, it still took the better part of 20 years to sell-through a few thousand cases of the stuff.

Because of the scattershot way A. H. Hirsch Reserve was managed, it probably didn't reward its owners as much as some of the long-aged whiskeys that came later. Now that the last of the A. H. Hirsch Reserve bourbon has disappeared into the bunkers (and mouths) of whiskey lovers, we should thank the bourbon gods that it ever happened at all.

In the United States, the bourbon renaissance began about 20 years ago and really picked up steam in the last decade. Export volume grew in 2011 for the fifth consecutive year at a double-digit rate. Nearly half of all American whiskey produced today is sold outside the USA., but domestic sales are growing too. Against all odds, American whiskey is hip again.

When the bourbon renaissance began, one of the drivers was the surfeit of excellent, very old, glut-era bourbon and rye available at what suddenly began to seem like very reasonable prices. The ages ran from 15 up to an astounding 25 years old. The popularity of those products finally pulled the last of the glut-era whiskey though the system. Except for a few stragglers left on the shelves of obscure liquor stores, the glut-era whiskey is all gone.

Not just the A. H. Hirsch. Everything.

Some of the glut era whiskey was good, some of it was great, and some of it was too woody, at least to my taste, and should never have been released. All of the A. H. Hirsch Reserve was truly exceptional and outstanding; rich, complex, robust, elegant, beautifully-balanced, and not too woody despite its extreme age. That's what was so remarkable about it, this fairly large stash of whiskey, from an unusual place, that was in remarkable condition for its age.

A. H. Hirsch Reserve Straight Bourbon Whiskey exhibits everything bourbon lovers love about bourbon: rich, dark, caramel and vanilla, chocolate and coffee, sweet but not too sweet, full-flavored but not heavy, balanced with just the right amount of smoke, and spices like anise and clove.

At 15- to 20-years-old, how can it not be woody? That's the mystery. Maybe it was the weather. Pennsylvania had some long, cold winters in the mid-70s. It can't be warehouse location. When barrels are put away, they go in lots to different parts of the maturation facility, 50 barrels here, 60 barrels there, deliberately spreading them throughout the system.

Maybe it was the travel. Most bourbon is made, aged, and bottled at pretty much the same place. If it has to be moved before bottling it's usually in stainless steel tanks or plastic totes, not wooden barrels. Travel is not usually considered a good thing, because it represents an extra expense and risk. The A. H. Hirsch Reserve bourbon got around, and often in the original wood.

Maybe it was oxidation. The whiskey used in the final bottling of the gold capsule 16-year-old was in stainless steel tanks for 12 years. It's not supposed to change in a sealed tank, but maybe it did, just a little and for the better.

By the way, the 5-star rating cited on the Preiss bottles was given by F. Paul Pacult in his magazine, *Spirit Journal,* which was established in 1991, not long after the first Hirsch release. The rating was given to one of those earlier releases and not specifically to the 2003 bottling.

There definitely is *something* special about the A. H. Hirsch Reserve bourbon. It has a buzz, a unique frisson all its own, but its uniqueness is subtle. It is richly flavorful and shockingly well-balanced. The long aging manifests itself as old leather, pipe tobacco, and dark fruit. It never goes over the top.

In my opinion, it is just about as good as bourbon gets, but not everyone agrees. Some find it so-so or actively dislike it. Some say the early releases were great but the 16-year-old gold foil release was crap.

Whiskey enthusiasts are like that. They never all line up behind anything.

Until it is preserved in glass (or stainless steel), whiskey is a living thing, always changing. The circumstances of this bourbon's life – made and mostly aged in Pennsylvania, shipped in wood to southern Ohio or Kentucky and briefly aged some more there –

are totally unique and had to have had some effect on the finished product. Did the sum of those conditions make it great? Impossible to say. All we know for sure is that the set of circumstances was unique and the whiskey, in the opinion of many, was great.

We know A. H. Hirsch Reserve was a rye-recipe bourbon, using a fairly standard mash bill of 75 percent corn, 13 percent rye and 12 percent malt. We know it was made with Beam yeast. Charles Everett Beam's daughter recalls her father asking his brothers to send him some yeast from Kentucky to get the Pennsylvania distillery going. Presumably, this was the same yeast Charles Everett Beam's father developed at the end of Prohibition. The Beams were always practical, not scientific distillers, who preserved and propagated their yeast with jug yeast.

After he retired from his day-to-day duties at Michter's in 1972, Everett Beam and his wife moved back to Kentucky, to a home on the south side of Louisville on the same block as their son. They never returned to Pennsylvania. A homebody, Everett liked to garden and cook, and occasionally went fishing in Canada. The fishing trips were always followed by a big family cook-out. A Roman Catholic, Charles Everett Beam was a fifth degree Knight of Columbus.

His wife, Alberta "Peachy" Beam died in 1986 after a long struggle with cancer and Charles Everett followed in 1989, dying quickly from a massive heart attack. They are buried next to his parents in Bardstown.

I never knew the 15-year-old and 18-year-old expressions of A. H. Hirsch Reserve even existed until Julian Van Winkle III gave me the run down of all the different bottlings, so I have not tasted them. I have tasted both the 19- and 20-year-old on several occasions, but not in a situation where I could contemplate them carefully or take detailed notes.

Suffice it to say that there isn't a lot of difference among the various expressions. There isn't much difference between the whiskey dumped at 16 and the whiskey that made it all the way to 20. Of course, the whiskey having been dumped at different times, in small batches, meant that each batch had its own personality, though undoubtedly Van Winkle and Hue did their best to maintain a uniform profile.

I have personally gone through several bottles of the 16-year-old gold capsule over the last nine years and still have one or two left. They are precious to me and I look forward to cracking them at some future date. I know they can't be replaced.

Although I consider the A. H. Hirsch bourbon to be one of the best whiskeys I've ever tasted, I wouldn't say it is *the* best. It is, however, in elite company. I have had several opportunities in the past to drink Very Very Old Fitzgerald, another legendary whiskey, though it has been a few years and, sadly, I have no bottles of that in my bunker. Just as precious as my A. H. Hirsch bottles are my remaining bottles of Old Commonwealth bourbon, a Van Winkle bottling of 10-year-old Stitzel-Weller wheated bourbon. I have an unopened bottle of Booker's Bourbon signed by Booker Noe that is precious for its provenance, a bottle of 10-year-old, 55% ABV Weller's from the early 1970s, a bottle of Pappy Van Winkle 23-year-old bottled about 10 years ago, and a couple bottles of medicinal whiskey.

Medicinal whiskey, distilled before 1920 and bottled between 1920 and 1933, can be easier to find than A. H. Hirsch Reserve Straight Bourbon Whiskey.

Not all of my precious bottles are ancients that you can't find today. I have about half a bottle of Abraham Bowman limited edition Virginia whiskey, a straight bourbon aged 18 years and released just last year, that I predict people will still be talking about many years from now. You can walk into any state store in Virginia and walk out with a bottle of it today. Several of the limited edition Four Roses Single Barrel bourbons have risen to the highest level, as have a few of the Old Forester Birthday Bourbons and just about any release of Heaven Hill's Parker's Heritage Collection. Outstanding bourbons, ryes and wheat whiskeys are released all the time.

These are the good old days.

So if you, in fact, never do taste any of the A. H. Hirsch Reserve bourbon, don't feel too bad. Write it off to an accident of birth. The time to be buying it was the late 1990s until about 2004. Then it was $50 and up, a lot for bourbon at the time. Now most of the people who bought it then wish they had bought more. I stopped when it got to $80.

The point is, even if you missed A. H. Hirsch Reserve, there are plenty of great bourbons out there and new ones are coming out all the time. Don't worry about what you missed ten years ago, worry about what you might be missing today. Go get them and in the future you'll be able to tell newbies about the whiskeys you've tasted that they will never have.

It's the cycle of life.

17. About The Author.

Charles K. Cowdery is a Kentucky Colonel (Patton, 206) and a member of the Kentucky Bourbon Hall of Fame (2009). He is the author of *BOURBON, STRAIGHT: The Uncut and Unfiltered Story of American Whiskey* and producer/director of the documentary "Made and Bottled in Kentucky."

He writes for Whisky Advocate, WHISKY Magazine, and other publications, and is editor and publisher of *The Bourbon Country Reader,* the only publication dedicated exclusively to American whiskey.

As a marketing professional, Cowdery has worked in and around the American liquor industry for more than 25 years, including nine in Kentucky. His other books include *Blues Legends,* 20 profiles of notable blues musicians. He does speaking appearances on both subjects, bourbon and blues.

Write to cowdery@ix.netcom.com for more information about private classes, tastings and personal appearances.

Cowdery is also a marketing writer for a variety of commercial clients, and an attorney. He lives in Chicago, Illinois.